Macmillan
ENCYCLOPEDIA
OF SCIENCE

8

Industry
Mining and Manufacturing

Robin Kerrod

Macmillan Publishing Company
New York

Maxwell Macmillan International Publishing Group
New York   Oxford   Singapore   Sydney

Published by:
Macmillan Publishing Company
A Division of Macmillan, Inc.
866 Third Avenue, New York, NY 10022

Collier Macmillan Canada, Inc.
1200 Eglinton Avenue East, Suite 200
Don Mills, Ontario M3C 3N1

Planned and produced by Andromeda Oxford Ltd.

Copyright © 1991 Andromeda Oxford Ltd.
Macmillan edition copyright © 1991 Macmillan Publishing Company

Library of Congress Cataloging-in-Publication Data

Macmillan encyclopedia of science.
          p.   cm.
          Includes bibliographical references and index.
          Summary: An encyclopedia of science and technology, covering
       such areas as the Earth, the ocean, plants and animals, medicine,
       agriculture, manufacturing, and transportation.
          ISBN 0-02-941346-X (set)
          1. Science–Encyclopedias, Juvenile.   2. Engineering–
       Encyclopedias, Juvenile.   3. Technology–Encyclopedias, Juvenile.
       [1. Science–Encyclopedias.   2. Technology–Encyclopedias.]
       I. Macmillan Publishing Company   90-19940
       Q121.M27   1991   CIP
       503 – dc20   AC

Volumes of the *Macmillan Encyclopedia of Science*
  1 *Matter and Energy* ISBN 0-02-941141-6
  2 *The Heavens* ISBN 0-02-941142-4
  3 *The Earth* ISBN 0-02-941143-2
  4 *Life on Earth* ISBN 0-02-941144-0
  5 *Plants and Animals* ISBN 0-02-941145-9
  6 *Body and Health* ISBN 0-02-941146-7
  7 *The Environment* ISBN 0-02-941147-5
  8 *Industry* ISBN 0-02-941341-9
  9 *Fuel and Power* ISBN 0-02-941342-7
 10 *Transportation* ISBN 0-02-941343-5
 11 *Communication* ISBN 0-02-941344-3
 12 *Tools and Tomorrow* ISBN 0-02-941345-1

Printed in the United States of America

Introduction

Industry relies on a wealth of materials – wood from trees, metals and other substances from minerals, and so on – to make its many products. This volume surveys both natural materials and artificial ones like plastics, and examines the ways they are used in manufacturing. Much of the information is presented in drawings and diagrams. They are well worth your attention.

To learn about a specific topic, start by consulting the Index at the end of the book. You can find all the references in the encyclopedia to the topic by turning to the final Index, covering all 12 volumes, located in Volume 12.

If you come across an unfamiliar word while using this book, the Glossary may be of help. A list of key abbreviations can be found on page 87. If you want to learn more about the subjects covered in the book, look at the Further Reading section.

Scientists tend to express measurements in units belonging to the "International System," which incorporates metric units. This encyclopedia accordingly uses metric units (with American equivalents also given in the main text). More information on units of measurement is on page 86.

Contents

Part One

Minerals and Materials

The early periods of history are named after the main materials people used for tools, utensils, implements, and weapons. Prehistoric peoples lived in a Stone Age. Their tools did not advance much until, about 3500 BC, they discovered how to smelt ores to make bronze, and they entered a Bronze Age. About 2,000 years later, they began producing iron, and an Iron Age began. In the mid-1800s the Steel Age began.

Steel is still the dominant metal today. Modern technology also uses dozens of other metals for thousands of different purposes. It also uses many nonmetallic materials – sand, salt, wood, and oil – as raw materials for manufacturing.

Most of the raw materials for making metals and manufacturing are taken from the ground as minerals. Part One looks at these raw materials and the methods we use to mine and process them.

◀ Wood is one of the most useful and versatile materials. It is used as fuel and in building, and is pulped to make paper and other products. It also goes to make products such as rayon and cellophane.

Earth's resources

Spot facts

• In 1869 an almost pure gold nugget weighing over 70 kg (150 lb.) was found at Moliagul, in the state of Victoria, Australia. It was named the Welcome Stranger.

• The largest diamond ever found weighed more than half a kilogram (1 lb.). It was discovered in Pretoria, South Africa, in 1905 and named the Cullinan. A gem called the Star of Africa was cut from it, and is now in the Royal Scepter of the British crown jewels.

• The oceans of the world hold some 1.35 billion cubic meters (47.7 billion cu.ft.) of water and contain enough salt to cover Europe to a depth of 5 km (3 mi.).

• A forest the size of Sweden must be cut down every year to supply the world with paper.

▶ Amid dramatic scenery in Utah, oil geologists are boring into the ground with drilling equipment during a seismic survey. In the borehole they will place an explosive charge. Shock waves from the explosion will be recorded after they are reflected from underground rocks.

Industry uses vast amounts of materials to produce the things we use in our everyday lives. These materials are in turn made from basic substances we call raw materials, which come from the land, the sea, and even the air. They form part of the Earth's natural resources. The most useful industrial materials by far are the metals, particularly iron and steel. We obtain metals by processing certain minerals, which we extract from rock. Other minerals are processed into chemicals for industry or used as they are. The forests represent another natural resource, yielding timber for construction and for making chemicals and plastics.

Mineral resources

Workable mineral deposits

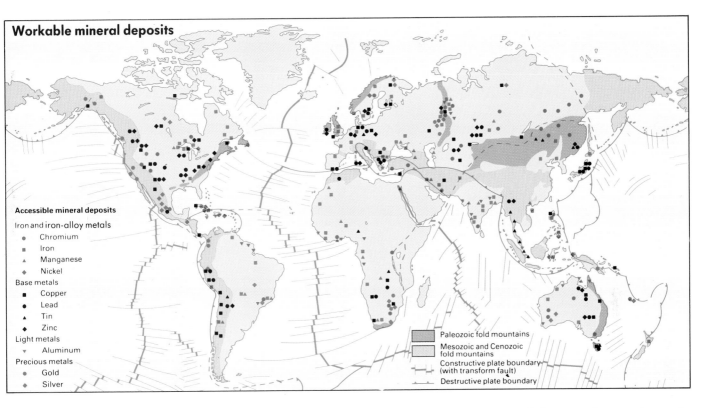

Accessible mineral deposits

Iron and iron-alloy metals
- ● Chromium
- ■ Iron
- ▲ Manganese
- ◆ Nickel

Base metals
- ■ Copper
- ● Lead
- ▲ Tin
- ◆ Zinc

Light metals
- ▼ Aluminum

Precious metals
- ● Gold
- ◆ Silver

Paleozoic fold mountains
Mesozoic and Cenozoic fold mountains
Constructive plate boundary (with transform fault)
Destructive plate boundary

▼ Junked cars waiting to be recycled. Recycling metals helps to conserve our precious mineral resources.

The Earth's crust, its solid outer layer, is made up of many kinds of rock. Every rock is made up of one or more minerals. Minerals are chemical compounds in which two or more elements are bonded together. Most minerals are made up of a metal combined with one or more nonmetals. For example, in the mineral cuprite, copper is combined with oxygen; in galena, lead is combined with sulfur. Copper and lead are metals; oxygen and sulfur are not.

The metal can be extracted from many of the minerals by simple chemical processing. However, it is worthwhile doing only where there are richer, or more concentrated, deposits of the minerals, known as ores.

The term "mineral resources" usually refers to those minerals found in ore deposits, which can be profitably worked to produce metals. The map above shows where in the world such deposits are to be found.

Note that ore deposits are not scattered evenly over the globe. They occur in regions where particular geological processes have been at work within the Earth. Many are found in regions where there are fold mountains, at the edges of some of the plates, or segments, that make up the Earth's crust.

9

Metallic minerals

People began using metals about 10,000 years ago. Copper, gold, and silver were the first metals to be used because they could be found in a native, or pure, form in the ground. But they were rare and were used mainly for making trinkets and jewelry. Some fine gold and silver jewelry has been recovered from ancient tombs in the Middle East. It is as beautiful as the day it was made, thousands of years ago.

The reason why gold and silver can be found in a native state and keep their beauty over a long period is that they are not very reactive. In other words, they do not readily combine with other chemical elements. They do not oxidize, or rust, in the way that iron does, for example.

Sometimes huge lumps, or nuggets, of native metals are found. Mostly, however, silver and gold are present in the rocks in specks. They become worth mining only when they have been concentrated into richer ore deposits.

Another important native metal, more precious than gold, is platinum. It is used in jewelry, and also in industry as a catalyst, a substance that speeds up chemical reactions. Platinum is usually found mixed with other metals, including palladium and osmium.

▶ A fascinating variety of copperware displayed in a French town. Copper is easily shaped by hammering.

◀ Gold leaf on the Massachusetts state capitol in Boston.

▼ Below, a small nugget of native gold.

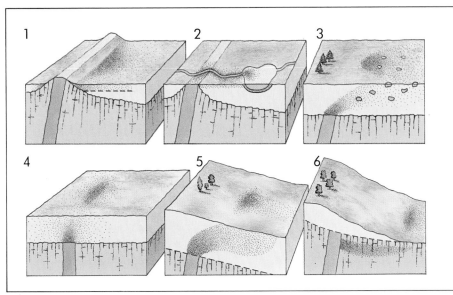

Mineral dispersion

Natural processes can scatter minerals over a wide area. The prevailing wind removes particles from an exposed vein (1). A river running through a vein carries particles away and deposits them downstream in the river bed (2). Glaciers may also erode and transport mineral deposits a long way from the vein (3). The action of water in the soil can break up and scatter minerals (4). So can the creep of soil down a slope (5), and the downward flow of groundwater (6), which can carry minerals away.

Ore minerals

Most metals are too reactive chemically to be found native in rock. They occur instead, combined with other elements, as minerals. When we can extract metals from these minerals, we call them ores.

Many ores are oxides, in which the metal is combined with oxygen. Most iron ores, such as magnetite, are oxides. The aluminum ore bauxite is an oxide. Also common are sulfide ores, in which the metal is combined with sulfur. The lead ore galena and the zinc ore sphalerite are both sulfides. The copper ores azurite and malachite are carbonates, the metal being combined with carbon and oxygen.

How ore deposits form

Various natural processes take place in the Earth's crust that concentrate minerals into workable ore deposits. For example, when molten rock, or magma, slowly cools deep underground, heavy minerals such as iron and chromium oxides tend to settle out first. The large magnetite deposits in Kiruna, Sweden, were formed in this way.

As the magma gradually becomes solid, a hot watery liquid remains which contains various minerals. This liquid works its way into cracks in the surrounding rocks and deposits the minerals as it cools. Such rich mineral veins, or lodes, are widely mined for such metals as copper, lead, zinc, and gold.

Other mineral deposits are formed as a result of processes which happen at the surface. Wind, rain, and frost slowly break down the rocks and free the minerals they contain. These may dissolve in rainwater and be carried by rivers into the sea. Sometimes sulfur compounds produced by decaying vegetation act on the dissolved matter and produce deposits of sulfides. The copper sulfide ores of Zambia, in Africa, were formed in this way.

▼ A well-shaped crystal of galena, the main ore of lead. It is the chemical compound lead sulfide. Like many metallic minerals, it has a metallic luster, or shine. The main deposits of galena are found in North and South America, Australia, Spain, and Germany.

Nonmetallic minerals

Nonmetals as well as metals can occur native in the Earth's crust. The chemical elements sulfur and carbon are examples. Sulfur fumes are given out by volcanoes. Vivid yellow deposits of sulfur can often be found around volcanic vents. Most sulfur, however, comes from processing pyrites, the mineral iron sulfide. Sulfur is a vital raw material for industry. It is made into sulfuric acid, one of the most widely used of all industrial chemicals.

Carbon appears in two quite different physical forms in nature. It occurs as black graphite, which is one of the softest of all minerals. It also occurs, more rarely, as transparent diamond. Diamond is the hardest of all minerals. When they are expertly cut, diamonds have a unique brilliance and sparkle, which makes them the most prized of all gems. Diamonds that are of too poor quality for gems are in demand in industry. Their extreme hardness makes them invaluable for grinding, polishing, and drilling work.

The most common nonmetallic mineral is quartz. Indeed, it is the most common mineral of all in the Earth's crust. It is a form of silica, or silicon dioxide. It is present in many rocks, such as granite, and it is the mineral which, finely divided, makes sand. Sand is used to make concrete, and also in glassmaking.

When quartz is very pure and transparent, it is called rock crystal. When attractively tinted, it forms gemstones, such as rose quartz and amethyst. Pearl opal is another precious form of silica, highly valued as a gem.

Sapphire and ruby are two other precious stones. They are rare forms of the mineral corundum, which is an oxide of aluminum. This mineral contains metal, but it is classed as a nonmetallic mineral because its use does not depend on the presence of the metal.

In a similar way calcite, a mineral form of calcium carbonate, is classed as nonmetallic. Calcite is found in large quantities in limestone and chalk rocks. Limestone has long been used as building stone. It is also used on a vast scale to make cement.

Most limestones were formed when seas containing dissolved calcium carbonate dried up, or evaporated. Such deposits are known as evaporites. Deposits of rock salt, sodium chloride, were formed in a similar way. Chalk has quite a different origin. It started out as dissolved calcium carbonate in the sea. This was used by microscopic organisms to build their chalky skeletons. When the organisms died, their skeletons built up over millions of years to form the thick chalk beds we find today. Such deposits are termed biogenic.

◀ The pyramids at Giza, in Egypt, are built of limestone blocks. The Great Pyramid of Khufu, completed about 2580 BC, is made up of over 2 million blocks. Some weigh as much as 15 metric tons. It is thought that several thousand workers toiled for 30 years or more on its construction. Limestone is a common building stone which can be cut readily. In modern cities limestone buildings are being attacked by acid rain.

Rock suits

When fire fighters move in to tackle a very hot fire, they wear fireproof suits made of rock. These suits are made from cloth woven from asbestos fibers.

Asbestos is the name given to various silicate minerals that form fibers. The most important of them are chrysotile and crocidolite. More than four million metric tons of asbestos are produced on average every year. Canada and the Soviet Union are the world's biggest producers. Asbestos is extracted at surface, or open-pit, mines.

Less than a third of the asbestos mined has fibers long enough to spin into yarn for making cloth. The rest is used, mixed with other materials, to make building materials and lagging for insulating boilers. Asbestos is mixed with cement, for example, to make pipes and roofing sheets. Its use in buildings, however, is now restricted because asbestos dust poses a health hazard. It causes a disease of the lungs called asbestosis.

▲ This hollow stone, called a geode, was found in Mexico. Millions of years ago a hot mineral-rich solution crystallized inside it, and this is the attractive result. Around the outside is blue agate. Inside are crystals of a purple-tinted variety of quartz called amethyst. Agate and quartz are different mineral forms of the chemical compound silica, or silicon dioxide. Both agate and amethyst are prized as gemstones.

◀ The Big Hole at Kimberley in South Africa. It was once the site of a rich diamond mine. The diamonds were found embedded in a carrot-shaped mass of heavy igneous rock formed from the Earth's upper mantle. It is called kimberlite, or blue ground.

13

Prospecting

Deposits of minerals are scattered far and wide throughout the world. Looking for mineral deposits is called prospecting. In the past many deposits were found by chance. Others were found by geologists looking in likely places for particular rocks they knew by experience might contain valuable minerals. Most of these obvious deposits of minerals have now been found and exploited. Most undiscovered deposits lie hidden beneath the surface rocks. Much more scientific methods of prospecting now have to be used to find them.

One of the first stages in prospecting these days is to examine images of the ground taken by satellites. These are called remote-sensing satellites because they carry sensors, or detectors, which look at the Earth's surface remotely, or from a distance. They can "see" not only in visible light, but also in light of other wavelengths such as infrared. At these other wavelengths they can often spot details of the landscape invisible in ordinary light.

Studying satellite images helps geologists select suitable areas to explore on the ground. They carry out tests with a variety of instruments to try to locate the kinds of rocks in which they think minerals might be found. They use such instruments as magnetometers, gravity meters, and Geiger counters.

Magnetometers measure the strength of a magnetic field. They indicate changes caused by the presence of mineral deposits, particularly those of magnetic iron ores, such as magnetite. Gravity meters detect slight changes in the Earth's gravity. This might indicate the presence of minerals with a different density from the surrounding rocks. Geiger counters pick up the radiation given off by radioactive substances. They are used when prospecting for the ores of radioactive metals such as uranium.

Geologists also take samples of rock and soil to analyze in the laboratory. This again may give them some clues about where mineral deposits can be found. They take samples from the surface and also drill deep into the rocks to get core samples. The large-scale structure of the underground rocks is investigated by means of a seismic survey.

▼ A Landsat image of Zimbabwe, in Africa, reveals the geology of the region. Landsat is a remote-sensing satellite, which takes pictures of the ground in light of different wavelengths. From the pictures, geologists are sometimes able to locate new mineral deposits.

A seismic survey

In a seismic survey, geologists set up vibrations in the ground called shock waves. Either they make an explosion or they use equipment that pounds the surface. As the waves travel downward, the rock layers refract (bend) or reflect them. The refracted or reflected waves travel back to the surface, where they are detected by sensitive instruments called geophones. From the way the waves are refracted or reflected, geologists can discover the structure of the rocks.

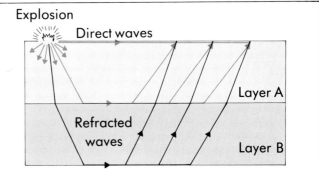

Explosion
Direct waves
Layer A
Refracted waves
Layer B

◄ These vehicles are used in seismic surveys. They are fitted with equipment that sets up vibrations in the ground. This method causes much less disturbance than using explosions.

A geological survey

When searching for underground deposits of minerals, geologists first study existing maps and reports about a likely-looking area (1). Then they look at aerial photographs (2) and satellite images which may enable them to pinpoint suitable rock formations. On the ground, geologists sample the rocks (3) and send them for analysis. Seismic testing (4) helps build up a picture of the structure of the underground rocks, while drilling (5) is done to sample them.

1

2

3

4

5

The oceans

Fluoride
Strontium
Boric acid
Bromide
Bicarbonate
Potassium

Calcium

Magnesium

Sulfate

Sodium

Chloride

Dissolved salts

Water

Seawater

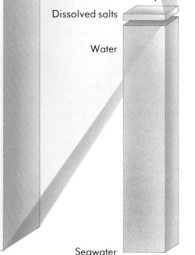

▲ This desalination plant in Saudi Arabia, in the Middle East, produces fresh water from the sea. It is an expensive process. The word desalination means "removing the salt from."

◀ There are about 35 parts of dissolved substances in every 1,000 parts of seawater. The column (left) shows the relative amounts of the main ones present.

More than two-thirds of the Earth's surface is covered by sea, to an average depth of nearly 4 km (over 2 mi.). It contains common salt, the chemical sodium chloride. It also contains the salts of many other metals as well. They include the chlorides, sulfates and carbonates of magnesium, potassium, and calcium.

The salts that are now dissolved in the sea came originally from rocks on the land. The action of the weather released minerals from the rocks into the rivers, and the rivers then carried them into the sea.

Seawater represents a vast storehouse of raw materials for the chemical industry. Common salt is already extracted from it on a large scale in many countries where the climate is hot. Much of the world's magnesium is obtained from seawater by electrolysis: passing electricity through it. Seawater is also the main source of the element bromine.

On the seabed in many parts of the ocean is another valuable resource, manganese nodules. These are rounded lumps of mineral matter that are rich in the metals manganese, copper, nickel, and cobalt. No one is sure how they form, but they are being produced at the rate of millions of metric tons a year.

The air

The air in the atmosphere is made up of a mixture of gases, mainly nitrogen, oxygen, and argon. In every 100 cubic meters (or cubic yards) of air there are 78 cubic meters (or cubic yards) of nitrogen, 21 of oxygen, and about 1 of the noble gas argon. In addition there are traces of helium, neon, krypton, and xenon.

The oxygen in the air takes part in every industrial process involving burning in air. Substances combine with oxygen when they burn. A major use for nitrogen is in the Haber process. This combines nitrogen with hydrogen to produce ammonia, used to make fertilizers and explosives.

Nitrogen and oxygen are also used in liquid form at very low temperatures. Liquid nitrogen (nitrogen below −196°C, or −320°F) is widely used as a freezing agent in industry. Liquid oxygen (−183°C, or −297°F) can be used as an explosive, and as a rocket propellant.

Liquid nitrogen and liquid oxygen are produced by the distillation of liquid air. Air itself is liquefied by the Linde process, named after the person who developed it. The process involves repeatedly compressing, cooling, and expanding the air. On each expansion, the temperature falls. Eventually it falls below the boiling point of air, and the air condenses, or turns into liquid. By carefully distilling the liquid it can be split up into the gases of which it is formed. Distilling liquid air is the main method of producing the noble gases.

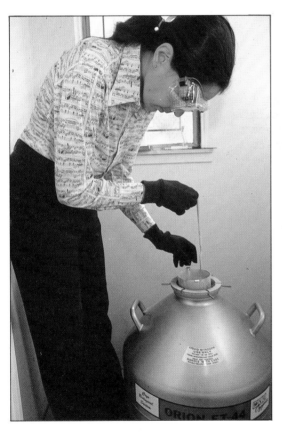

▲ This flask is cooled to very low temperatures by liquid nitrogen. It is used to store samples of human sperm. Sperm can be kept in this way for long periods.

▶ The space shuttle blasts off from the launch pad at the Kennedy Space Center in Florida. The main orbiter engines burn liquid hydrogen and liquid oxygen propellants.

The forest

From the earliest times, the wood from trees has been one of the most useful and versatile materials people have used. It is used as a fuel, and as a material to build houses and make furniture. It has also been used for more than a century to make wood pulp. Most wood pulp is made into paper. Some provides the starting point for a range of other useful materials, such as rayon fibers, cellophane film, and other cellulose products.

Apart from wood, trees produce many other useful substances. These include rubber, which is made from the sap of rubber trees. Solvents for paints can be made from the resin that oozes from the bark of pine trees.

Softwoods

About a third of the Earth's land surface is covered with forests. The two most heavily forested regions are the boreal (northern) forests of the Northern Hemisphere and the tropical rain forests, centered on the Equator.

The boreal forests are made up of conifer trees, which have needlelike leaves and bear their seeds in cones. Most conifers are evergreens, which never lose all their leaves at once. Their timber is generally quite soft and easy to work. For this reason, they are known as softwoods. Firs, pines, and spruces are examples. Softwood timber is the main raw material for wood pulp and the construction industry.

Hardwoods

By contrast, the timber from trees of the tropical rain forests is usually hard. For this reason the trees are called hardwoods. Ebony, teak, and mahogany are examples. These trees have broad leaves and are never bare, because they lose only a few leaves at a time. In some countries, these trees are protected.

Other kinds of hardwoods grow between the tropical and boreal forest regions. They are mainly deciduous trees, those that shed all their leaves in the autumn. Examples are ash, oak, birch, beech, and sycamore. Tropical and deciduous hardwoods are used for making furniture, flooring, and paneling.

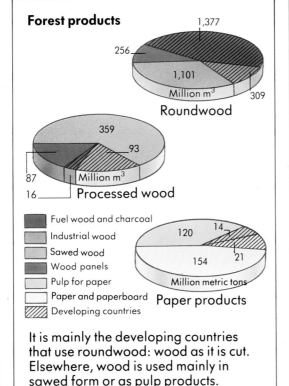

Forest products

Roundwood (Million m³): 1,377 — 256 — 1,101 — 309

Processed wood (Million m³): 359 — 93 — 87 — 16

Legend:
- Fuel wood and charcoal
- Industrial wood
- Sawed wood
- Wood panels
- Pulp for paper
- Paper and paperboard
- Developing countries

Paper products (Million metric tons): 120 — 14 — 154 — 21

It is mainly the developing countries that use roundwood: wood as it is cut. Elsewhere, wood is used mainly in sawed form or as pulp products.

◀ A timber mill in British Columbia, Canada. Logs felled in the surrounding forests are floated to the mill in the form of huge rafts. At the mill, they are sawed into standard lengths and thicknesses for the timber trade. These forests form part of the great belt of coniferous or evergreen forest that girdles the Northern Hemisphere. Most of the trees, such as spruces (inset), have a conical shape. This helps them shed snow better.

▲ A forest scientist tends seedlings at a tree nursery in Ghana, in West Africa. The seedlings have been raised as part of a selective breeding program to produce trees with more desirable characteristics, such as faster growth, a better yield of timber, and more resistance to disease. The seedlings will be transplanted to plots in the forest. The seeds of the best trees will then be used in further experiments.

Mining

Spot facts

• The Western Deep Levels gold mine in South Africa is the world's deepest mine, with shafts extending down nearly 4 km (over 2 mi.) below the surface.

• The temperature at the lowest point in the Western Deep Levels mine is 55°C (131°F), far hotter than in the hottest deserts on the surface.

• The Bingham Canyon copper mine, near Salt Lake City, Utah, is the world's largest open-pit mine. It covers an area of over 7 square kilometers (almost 3 sq. mi.) and has been excavated to a depth of nearly 800 meters (2,600 ft.).

• More than 10 million metric tons of salt are extracted from seawater by evaporation every year.

► This huge dredger removes cassiterite from an artificial lagoon in Malaysia, in Southeast Asia. Cassiterite is the ore from which tin is produced. It is found in large quantities around the Malay Peninsula.

Our early ancestors began digging materials from the ground in prehistoric times. So mining can be considered the earliest industry. Prehistoric people mined flint to make tools. Mining became more important about 6,000 years ago when we learned how to extract metals from ores in order to make tools. As the need for materials, especially metals, grew, so mining activities expanded. Today something like 50 billion metric tons of materials are removed from the Earth's crust by mining every year. Seven out of every ten tons come from surface, or open-pit, mines. The rest is extracted from underground mines or by using special methods, such as evaporating seawater. As natural resources become scarcer, we are having to mine in ever more remote areas.

Placer mining

In regions where the rocks contain gold, particles of the metal in time become dislodged under the action of the weather. Streams wash them away, but they eventually settle out in the stream bed because they are so heavy. They form deposits known as placers.

During the great "gold rushes" of the 1800s in California, Canada, and Australia, people made fortunes by mining gold in placer deposits. The traditional method of doing this was panning: swirling around the gravel in a pan. The swirling action let any gold particles separate out and fall to the bottom. Further swirling then washed away the light, unwanted gravel, leaving the heavy gold "dust" behind.

When working on a larger scale, miners washed the gravel through troughs called sluice boxes. These were lined with sheep fleeces or felt, which trapped the gold dust as it settled out. A similar method is still used in some gold-mining areas. Miners use a water gun (a "hydraulic giant") to break up gold-bearing gravel and wash it into troughs. Here, grooved devices called riffles trap the gold.

Dredging

On a very much larger scale still, gold is extracted from stream beds by dredging. This method is also used widely to mine cassiterite, or tin ore. This ore is unusually heavy, which makes it possible to mine by placer methods.

The dredgers used for mining in water are great floating ore-processing plants, which can handle as much as 15,000 metric tons of gravel a day. The most common type is the bucket dredger. It has digging buckets in an endless chain mounted on a boom, which angles down into the water to reach the gravel bed.

The mined materials are sieved, or screened, and the finer material is washed over riffles, where the heavy ore or metal settles out. The unwanted material passes through the dredger and is usually dumped on the bank as spoil.

A great deal of gold is also mined underground. Over the years the spoil from the mines has built up into huge heaps. Because extraction methods have improved, these spoil heaps have now become a valuable source of gold.

▲ A miner in northwest Pakistan searches for gold in a river bed using a traditional method, a variation on panning. He pours a mixture of gravel and water onto a makeshift sieve. Particles of gold are washed into the pan underneath, where they settle out because they are heavier than the other mineral matter.

▶ A huge pile of spoil, or waste, at a South African gold mine. The spoil was discarded during early and less efficient mining operations and still contains a significant amount of gold, which could not be recovered at the time. It is now a major source of the metal. High-pressure hoses are used to break it up and wash it into processing plants, which dissolve out the gold by treatment with cyanide.

Open-pit mining

Mineral ores are easiest to mine when they lie on or near the surface of the ground. Then they are extracted by the open-pit method. Minerals mined in this way include iron ores, bauxite (aluminum ore), copper ores, and asbestos.

Open-pit mines are by far the largest mines. At the huge Bingham Canyon copper mine in Utah, some 90,000 metric tons of ore are mined each day. Some 3.5 billion metric tons of material have been removed since it opened.

The overburden
In a typical open-pit mine, the ore deposits lie beneath a layer of unwanted soil or rock. This is called the overburden, and has to be stripped away before mining can begin. This is done by huge excavating machines. One is the bucket-wheel excavator, which has a rotating wheel with digging buckets mounted around the edge. Another is the walking dragline, so called because of its unusual method of motion. Some of these machines can cast their digging bucket 100 meters (over 100 yd.) and scoop up more than 50 cubic meters (65 cu. yd.) of material at a time.

After the overburden has been removed, the ore body, if it is hard, must be broken up with explosives. Then it is loaded by mechanical shovels into railroad cars or trucks.

Surface deposits of china clay are so soft that they can be broken up by water jets and then washed into treatment plants.

Quarrying building stone

Stone such as limestone, marble, and granite has been used for building since the early days of civilization. The Great Pyramids of Egypt, for example, are built of limestone blocks. The famous Taj Mahal at Agra, in northern India, is built of pure white marble. White marble from quarries at Carrara, in Italy (pictured above), were used by the great sculptors Michelangelo and Leonardo da Vinci.

In a quarry workers split the stone carefully using the natural "grain" of the rock. In hard rock such as granite they drill holes in a line and then drive in wedges. In softer rock such as limestone they cut a groove in the stone by machine. Blocks may also be cut by wire saws.

▼ A huge power shovel loads an ore train at the Valdivia nitrate mine in northern Chile, South America. Chile has one of the world's largest deposits of sodium nitrate, otherwise known as Chile saltpeter.

▶ An open-pit mine in Colorado, producing molybdenite, the main ore of the metal molybdenum. The picture shows the vast scale of open-pit operations, which can extend over many square kilometers.

Underground mining

The ores of iron, aluminum, and copper, for example, are often found on or near the surface and can be extracted by open-pit mining. However, most metal ores are found locked in the rock underground. Some are found in quite large deposits, others only as relatively thin veins running between the rock layers. The deposits may be horizontal or slope at any angle, following the angle of the rock layers.

A mineral vein may show itself at the surface as an outcrop. But usually it is detected indirectly from geological investigations. These include seismic tests and measurements by such instruments as magnetometers, gravity meters, and Geiger counters. If the signs are good, then holes are drilled into the rock to produce core samples: cylinders that give a cross section of the rock layers. If ore is reached, it is assessed chemically for its metal content.

Geologists then try to work out how far the ore body extends.

The cost of mining

To justify underground mining, there must be enough ore to make it worthwhile. This is because the cost of underground mining is very high compared with that of surface mining. The cost of boring shafts and tunnels is high. So is the cost of making an underground mine into a place safe enough for miners to work.

In a typical mine, a main shaft is sunk vertically into the ground. Then tunnels are dug horizontally out from it at various levels to reach the ore deposit. An elevator, or cage, is installed in the shaft to carry the miners between the surface and the working levels. A hoist, or skip, lifts the ore to the surface.

As mining progresses, the tunnels lengthen.

Railways then need to be laid to transport the miners and ore between the shaft and working face. In some mines the ore is transported by conveyors. The world's largest underground mine has a network of tunnels totaling more than 560 km (350 mi.) in length. It is the San Manuel copper mine in Arizona.

For safety, the shafts must be lined and the tunnels supported in areas where the rock is weak. Ventilation equipment must be installed to keep the miners supplied with fresh air and to remove dust and potentially dangerous gases. In coal mines in particular, methane gas, often called firedamp, can seep from the rocks. This forms an explosive mixture with air that can be set off by a spark. In particularly deep mines, the air also needs to be refrigerated because the temperature increases with depth.

In underground mining, miners generally use explosives to break up and remove the ore from the rock. First, "shot holes" are drilled in the rock face to take the explosive charges. Hand-held pneumatic hammer drills may be used. They are rather like the jackhammers used in breaking up pavement and work by compressed air. Sometimes a number of drills may be mounted on a wheeled frame called a jumbo to drill many holes at once.

The space from which ore is removed is called a stope. Often ore is removed by the room-and-pillar method. Pillars of ore are left here and there during mining to support the roof of the excavation. Later, the pillars themselves may be recovered, allowing the roof to cave in.

Because coal is soft enough to be cut, semi-automatic machines can be used to remove it. Coal is the decayed remains of huge plants that grew hundreds of millions of years ago.

▲ Working in a salt mine in Kewra, Pakistan. Usually, the salt deposit is broken up by explosives and then loaded mechanically into railway cars for removal. Deposits are often many meters thick.

◄ A miner uses a compressed-air jackhammer to bore a shot hole in the ore face in an African mine. Electric drills are not used underground here because of the danger that sparks will set off any explosive gases present. After drilling, an explosive charge will be placed in the hole and detonated to break up the ore body. The broken rock will then be transported by skip.

▲ A sharp-toothed mechanical shearer slices through the coal face in an underground mine. It travels along the face, ripping out the coal, which is removed by a chain conveyor. The shearer works under the protection of "walking" props. These are metal roof supports that move forward as the coal face is cut back. Water from the cutting head lubricates, cools, and lays the dust.

Other extraction methods

Apart from the traditional open-pit and underground mining methods, there are others that have been developed to extract particular minerals. For example, petroleum, or crude oil, is extracted by drilling. Drilling also plays a role in borehole mining, used to extract minerals such as salt and sulfur. The minerals in seawater can be removed by solar evaporation, using the heat of the Sun. Techniques of removing minerals from the deep seabed are also being investigated.

Drilling

Oil is found trapped in the rock layers. It can be detected from the surface by such methods as seismic surveying. It is reached by holes bored by rotary drills. The drilling takes place from drilling rigs about 60 m (200 ft.) tall. A drill bit, with rotating cutting wheels, is attached to the end of a drill pipe. The pipe is gripped and turned by a device called the rotary table.

As the bit bores deeper, more and more lengths of pipe have to be added. When the bit has to be changed, the whole string of pipes is raised by the lifting gear high up in the rig. Mud is pumped down through the hollow drill pipes to lubricate the wheels of the bit and to bring back the rock cuttings.

The borehole is usually lined with steel pipes as it deepens. If oil is struck (and often it is not), the hole is capped with a "Christmas tree." This is a complex of valves and tubes from which the oil can be extracted at a controlled rate.

There is such a demand for oil that deposits are being tapped in the remotest places, such as the bitterly cold Arctic. Offshore drilling is done

▶ (main picture) An oil drilling rig in the far north of Alaska, where temperatures may plummet to −50°C (−58°F) and below. The floor of the drill rig is enclosed and heated to protect the operators. Oil began to flow in large quantities from Alaska in 1977, when the Trans-Alaska Pipeline was completed.
(inset) A close-up of activity at a drilling rig. The drill bit needs changing, and hundreds of meters of pipe have to be extracted first from the borehole.

▲ This chemical plant in Israel extracts salt and other minerals from the water. The seawater is first pumped into large ponds to allow impurities to settle out. Then it passes to crystallization pans, where the water evaporates. Salt and other minerals are deposited.

by drill ships or semisubmersible rigs. The oil is extracted from massive production platforms that rest on or are pinned by piles to the seabed.

Borehole mining

Traditionally, the mining of rock salt takes place by normal underground mining methods. But at many salt mines these days the salt is extracted differently. A hole is drilled down to the underground deposit, and then water is pumped in. The salt dissolves in the water to form a strong solution of brine. Then the brine is pumped back to the surface. The water is then evaporated off by heating, and the salt separates out.

Sulfur is mined by a similar method, called the Frasch process after the man who developed it. This process uses three pipes of different diameters, one inside the other. Water is heated above its boiling point and pumped down into the deposit through the outer and middle pipes. This causes the sulfur to melt.

Then after about a day, the supply of water to the middle pipe is stopped, and air is forced at high pressure down the inner pipe. This forces a frothy mixture of molten sulfur and hot water up through the middle pipe to the surface. The mixture goes into settling tanks, where the sulfur settles out nearly 100 percent pure.

Deep-water mining

Many valuable minerals and metals, including common salt, potash, and magnesium, are extracted from seawater by evaporation or electrolysis. Other valuable minerals are present on the deep seabed in the form of manganese nodules. They can be mined using a suction method. Further development awaits new technologies and international agreements over the mining rights to such deposits.

Mineral processing

Spot facts

- Over 700 million metric tons of steel are produced every year in the world, nearly 50 times as much as aluminum, the next most useful metal.

- A blast furnace operates continuously for months at a time, and can produce 8,000 metric tons or more of pig iron every 24 hours.

- Deadly cyanide poison is often used to extract gold from its ores.

- Several tons of some uranium ores have to be processed to produce a kilogram (about 2 lb.) of the metal.

► Red-hot molten steel pouring from a converter at a steelworks. It takes only about three-quarters of an hour for a converter-full of pig iron from a blast furnace to be refined into steel.

A few minerals, such as diamonds and native gold, can be used more or less as they are dug from the ground. But the majority of minerals need to be processed in some way before we can use them. Most mineral ores, for example, have to be heated to high temperatures in a furnace before they yield metals. Metals can be extracted from some ores by passing electricity through them. Furnace methods are also used to process many nonmetallic minerals. Limestone, sand, and clay, for example, are burned, or "fired," to produce a wide range of ceramic products, such as pottery, bricks, and cement.

Smelting the ore

A common method of extracting metals from their ores is by heating them in a furnace to high temperatures. This process is called smelting. Iron, for example, is made by smelting iron ore in a blast furnace.

Most iron ores are oxides, in which the iron is combined with oxygen. The main object of smelting is to remove this oxygen. Any "earthy" impurities in the ore must also be removed.

Iron ore is loaded, or charged, into the furnace with coke and limestone. The coke burns and heats the furnace to a temperature of up to 1,600°C (2,900°F). It also reacts chemically with the iron ore. Coke is mainly carbon, and it combines with the oxygen in the ore to form carbon monoxide gas, which escapes. The iron is left behind. Because of the high temperature, it is molten. It trickles down and collects in the base of the furnace, or hearth.

Meanwhile, the impurities in the ore combine with the added limestone. They form a liquid called slag. This too runs down to the hearth and settles as a layer on top of the molten iron. From time to time the furnace is opened, or tapped, to extract the slag and iron.

Years ago the molten iron ran into a trough and from there into small molds. These molds were called pigs, since they were side by side like piglets feeding from a sow. The iron became known as pig iron, and the term is still used. Today, however, most pig iron is fed into huge traveling ladles, which carry it directly to the steelmaking furnaces. In these furnaces the iron is further purified, or refined.

Blast furnaces are also used to smelt other metals, including lead. Lead ore cannot be smelted as it is because it is a sulfide: the metal is combined with sulfur. First it has to be roasted in air. This changes it to an oxide, which the furnace can handle.

Most ores contain a good deal of earth and rock, called gangue. As much of this as possible must be removed before smelting. Methods of removing the gangue, and concentrating the ore, are known as mineral dressing. They use differences in such properties as density or magnetism to separate the ore from the gangue. Flotation is one useful method.

▼ Steel scrap at a quay in Florida. Large amounts of steel scrap are added with pig iron to steelmaking furnaces. The scrap is carefully selected, so that the resulting steel will have the right composition.

Flotation

In this method of mineral dressing, the ore is finely crushed and fed into a bath of water, to which an oil or chemical has been added. When air is bubbled through the bath, particles of ore attach themselves to the bubbles and form a scum on top. This is then skimmed off. Gangue particles remain behind.

Iron into steel

Pig iron is produced when iron ore is smelted with coke and limestone in a blast furnace. It is not pure iron, but contains a lot of impurities, particularly carbon (about 4 percent). This makes the iron brittle. Only when most of the carbon is removed does the metal become really useful. It then becomes steel.

Steel is the name we give to the alloy, or mixture, of iron with traces of carbon. The presence of just a few parts per thousand of carbon makes iron much stronger and harder than it is when pure.

In steelmaking, the excess carbon is literally burned out of the pig iron in a furnace. Most steel is now made by the basic oxygen method. The carbon burns off when a jet of oxygen is blasted into the molten pig iron. The highest quality steel is made by melting selected steel scrap in an electric-arc furnace. Heat is produced in this furnace by an electric arc, a kind of continuous electric spark.

Steelworks are vast. They not only produce the metal, but also carry out many shaping processes, such as rolling, forging, and casting.

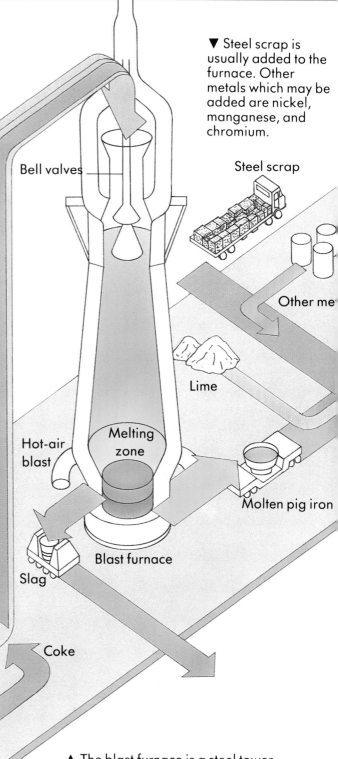

▼ Steel scrap is usually added to the furnace. Other metals which may be added are nickel, manganese, and chromium.

Steel scrap

Other me

Lime

Bell valves

Hot-air blast

Melting zone

Molten pig iron

Blast furnace

Slag

Coke

▼ Iron ore is made into pellets or mixed with coke and limestone to form lumpy "sinter."

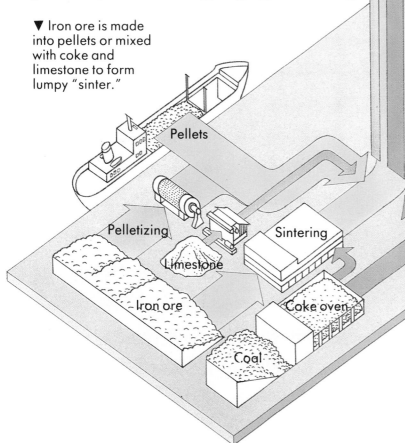

Pellets

Pelletizing

Sintering

Limestone

Iron ore

Coke oven

Coal

▲ The blast furnace is a steel tower, standing about 60 m (200 ft.) high and measuring 10 m (over 30 ft.) in diameter. Iron ore, coke, and limestone are charged into the top of the furnace through a "double-bell" valve system. This prevents the loss of the furnace gases, which include carbon monoxide. The gases are burned as fuel in "stoves." These stoves heat the air which is blasted into the base of the furnace.

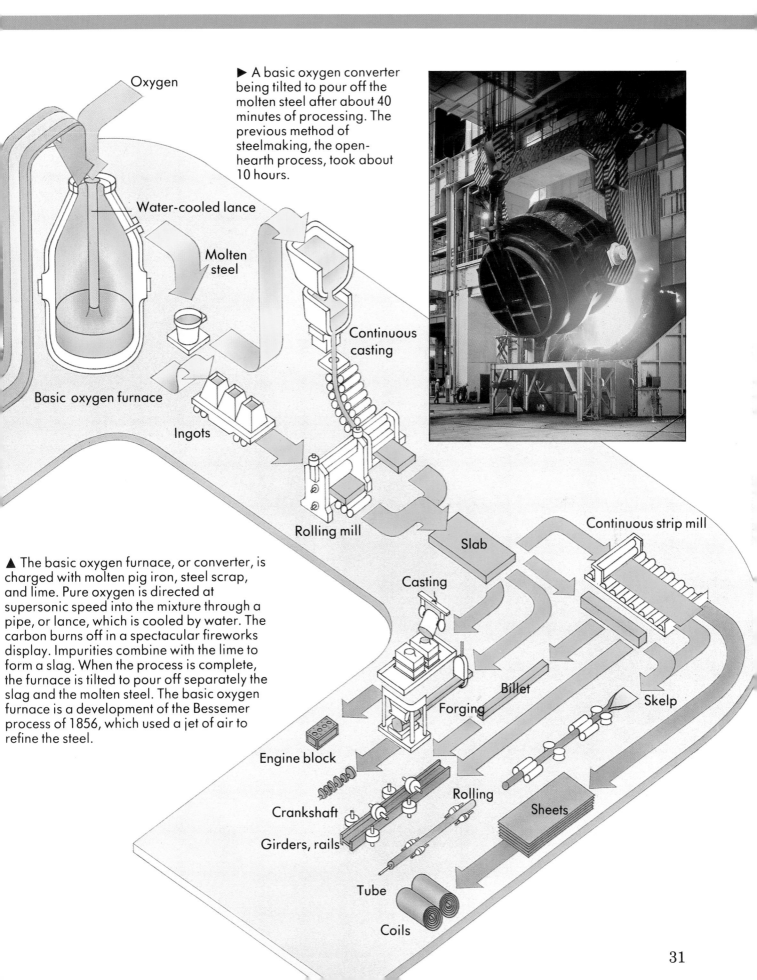

Oxygen

▶ A basic oxygen converter being tilted to pour off the molten steel after about 40 minutes of processing. The previous method of steelmaking, the open-hearth process, took about 10 hours.

Water-cooled lance

Molten steel

Basic oxygen furnace

Continuous casting

Ingots

Rolling mill

▲ The basic oxygen furnace, or converter, is charged with molten pig iron, steel scrap, and lime. Pure oxygen is directed at supersonic speed into the mixture through a pipe, or lance, which is cooled by water. The carbon burns off in a spectacular fireworks display. Impurities combine with the lime to form a slag. When the process is complete, the furnace is tilted to pour off separately the slag and the molten steel. The basic oxygen furnace is a development of the Bessemer process of 1856, which used a jet of air to refine the steel.

Slab

Casting

Continuous strip mill

Billet

Skelp

Forging

Engine block

Crankshaft

Rolling

Sheets

Girders, rails

Tube

Coils

Producing other metals

Lead, zinc, and tin are smelted in blast furnaces in a similar way to iron. Some metals are produced in different kinds of furnaces. Others are extracted by means of electrolysis; this is known as electrometallurgy. Electrolysis is also widely used for purifying metals that may have been extracted by other methods. The extraction of copper from different ores provides a good illustration of these alternative methods.

Copper smelting

Copper often occurs in sulfide ores, in which it is combined with other metals, particularly iron and nickel. The presence of these other metals complicates the extraction process. The follow-

ing smelting processes are used for the ore chalcopyrite, or copper pyrites, which is a mixed sulfide of copper and iron.

The ore is first concentrated by flotation and then smelted in a reverberatory furnace. Flames shoot over the concentrate and turn it into a bubbling, boiling mass. Some of the iron ore and impurities together form a slag, which is run off. What remains is matte, a mixture of copper and iron sulfides.

The matte is transferred to another furnace, called a converter, and air is blown through it. Sand (silica) is added, which absorbs the iron and other impurities. This results in blister copper, which is about 98 percent pure.

Smelting aluminum

Aluminum is produced by the electrolysis of molten aluminum oxide. The principle is simple, but the practice is complicated. First, the aluminum oxide must be extracted from bauxite, the ore of aluminum.

This is done by the Bayer process, in which the bauxite is digested with caustic soda (sodium hydroxide). The aluminum oxide dissolves to form sodium aluminate. Crystals of aluminum hydroxide form when the aluminate is cooled. These are filtered off and then heated. This process (calcination) produces alumina (aluminum oxide).

Alumina by itself does not melt until it reaches about 2,000°C (3,600°F). Mixed with a mineral called cryolite, it will melt at only about 1,000°C (1,800°F). In aluminum smelting, a mixture of alumina and cryolite is charged into the furnace. In the furnace, carbon rods (the anodes) are lowered into the molten mixture. Electricity passes between them and the carbon furnace lining (the cathode). The electricity splits up the aluminum oxide into aluminum metal, which collects as a molten layer on the floor of the furnace. Oxygen combines with the carbon anodes to form carbon monoxide, which is led off.

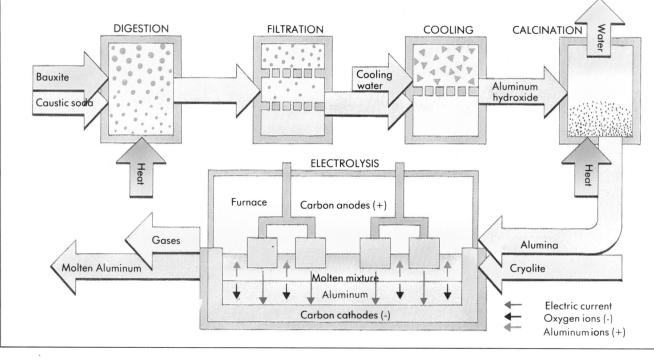

Electrolysis

The purification of the copper is completed by electrolysis – passing electricity through a solution. The impure copper is made into blocks, which become the anodes (positive electrodes) in the process. Sheets of pure copper become the cathodes (negative electrodes). They are placed in a bath of copper sulfate solution, and an electric current is passed through them.

Under the influence of the electricity, copper from the impure anode goes into solution as ions (charged atoms). Pure copper comes out of solution at the cathode, where copper ions change back into atoms. The result is that the anodes dissolve away, while the cathodes grow. Impurities settle out as a slime.

Leaching

The electrolysis of copper sulfate also plays an important part in the extraction of copper from oxide ores, such as cuprite. The ores are treated with sulfuric acid, which dissolves the copper as copper sulfate. This kind of process is called leaching. It is an example of hydrometallurgy, the extraction of metals by means of chemical solutions.

Leaching is also an important method of removing uranium, gold, and silver from low-grade ores, which contain only the minutest amounts of metal. Uranium is also extracted by treatment with sulfuric acid. Gold and silver are removed from their ores using a weak solution of sodium cyanide.

▲ Molten zinc being tapped from a furnace. Zinc is smelted in a blast furnace, which it leaves as a vapor because of its quite low melting point. Molten metal forms when the vapor is cooled.

▼ The copper in some ores is removed by treatment with sulfuric acid (left). The copper sulfate that forms is then reduced to copper metal by electrolysis. Copper is deposited on the cathode plates of the electrolytic bath (below), which holds the copper sulfate solution. It is deposited as very pure copper.

Metals and alloys

Altogether in nature, there exist about 90 chemical elements, which are the basic "building blocks" of matter. Seventy of them are metals. The metals we are most familiar with, such as iron and steel, aluminum, copper, and nickel, are tough, strong, and quite dense substances. But not all metals are like this. The metal sodium is so soft that it can be cut with a knife. The metal mercury is a liquid at ordinary temperatures. Mercury is the silvery liquid you can see in some thermometers.

All these metals are shiny and pass on, or conduct, heat and electricity well. But we cannot define a metal in this way because some nonmetals (such as arsenic) look metallic and others (such as carbon) conduct electricity well.

The scientist defines a metal as an element which, in solution, forms ions with a positive electric charge. Ions are atoms which have lost or gained electrons. The only nonmetal that forms positive ions in solution is hydrogen.

Metal properties

Every metal has individual properties that set it apart from the others. For example, iron is magnetic and rusts, or corrodes, easily in moist air. Gold is not magnetic and never corrodes, keeping its shiny appearance century after century. It is not attacked by acids, as other metals are. Only a mixture of concentrated nitric and hydrochloric acids will attack it.

Lead is very soft at ordinary temperatures. Chromium is very hard. Aluminum softens in temperatures of a few hundred degrees. Tungsten will not soften until the temperature rises to several thousand degrees. Cast iron is very brittle and snaps easily. Copper, however, can be bent double without snapping. Copper can also be stretched into a fine wire nearly as thin as a hair without breaking. We say it is a very ductile metal. Gold can be hammered into a very thin sheet without breaking up. We say it is very malleable.

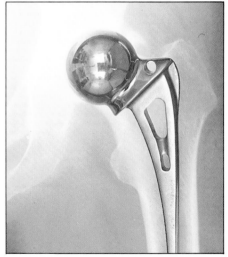

▲ This artificial hip joint is made from titanium and a chromium-cobalt alloy. It is immensely strong and, what is very important, it does not react with body tissues. Stainless steel is another alloy used for implants.

◄ Engineers checking out a turbofan engine. Jet engines are constructed of special alloys that keep their strength at high temperatures. They contain such metals as titanium, nickel, and tungsten.

Alloys

▲ A graceful bronze statue in a public garden in southern England. Bronze is easy to cast in molds because it flows easily when molten. Bronze does not readily corrode in damp conditions, and so it is an ideal material for outdoor statues and monuments.

Strange as it may seem, most metals are not used in our everyday world in their pure form. In general, pure metals are too weak and too soft to be of use in industry. However, the properties of a metal can often be greatly improved by adding to it traces of another metal or nonmetal. Soft and weak iron, for example, is transformed by the addition of traces of carbon into the hard, strong metal we call steel. The weak metals copper and zinc become the strong metal brass when they are mixed.

Steel and brass are metal mixtures we call alloys. Most metals are used in the form of alloys, which are almost always stronger and harder than the metals they are made from.

Metals are also alloyed to improve their chemical properties. Nickel and chromium are metals that do not corrode. When they are added to steel, which by itself does rust, they make the steel rustproof too. The resulting alloy is stainless steel, one of our most widely used alloys. Nickel and chromium are also the main alloying elements in the heat-resistant Nichrome series of alloys used in jet engines. One very interesting nickel-iron alloy is called Invar. Unlike other metals, it scarcely expands or contracts at all when heated or cooled.

Copper is used in a wide variety of alloys. With tin, it makes bronze; with nickel, it makes cupronickel. Both alloys are used for coins. Small traces of copper and other metals are added to aluminum. This soft, weak metal is transformed into an alloy as strong as steel, yet only one-third as dense. This alloy, called duralumin, is almost always used in building aircraft, which must be as light as possible.

Ceramics

Clay was one of the first natural materials used on a large scale. People began using it to make pottery at least 9,000 years ago. They shaped moist clay into pots, bowls, and other vessels. Then they baked them hard, first in an open fire and later in a special oven, or kiln.

Pottery is produced in much the same way today, although industrially the process is on a vast scale. It is the most familar example of ceramics. Ceramics are products made by baking clay or other nonmetallic materials in a kiln or furnace. Bricks, cement, glass, and refractories are other examples.

Pottery

The ordinary kind of pottery we use every day is called earthenware. It is made from cheap clays and is baked, or fired, at a relatively low temperature (about 1,000°C, or 1,800°F). It is dull in texture and lets water through. To make it waterproof, it has to be glazed.

The finest pottery, porcelain, is made from pure white china clay. It is fired at a high temperature (about 1,400°C, or 2,500°F), to make it glasslike and waterproof. Porcelain is used widely in the electrical industry because it is an excellent insulator.

Cement and concrete

Cement binds the ingredients of concrete together. It is made by roasting such materials as clay and chalk or limestone at about 1,400°C (2,500°F) in a rotating kiln. The raw materials are fed to the kiln in the form of a slurry, a mixture with water, or as a moist "cake" or a dry "meal." Lumps called clinker emerge from the kiln. Dust is removed by a precipitator and returned to the clinker. Materials such as gypsum may then be added, and the whole mixture is then ground finely in a rotating ball mill.

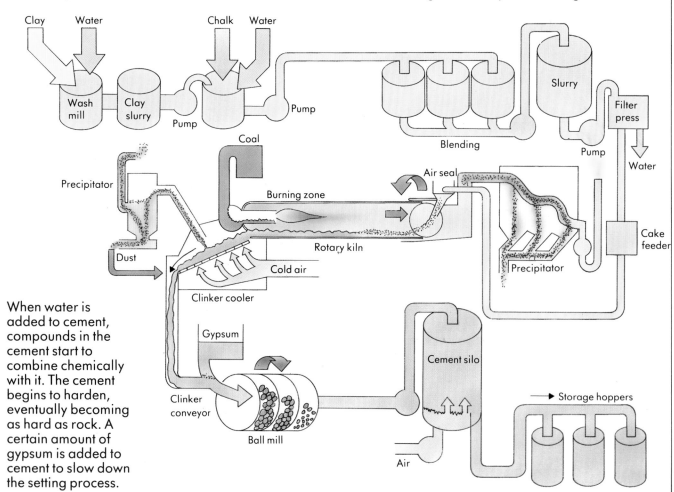

When water is added to cement, compounds in the cement start to combine chemically with it. The cement begins to harden, eventually becoming as hard as rock. A certain amount of gypsum is added to cement to slow down the setting process.

Glass

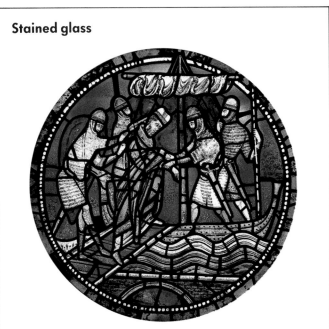

The art of producing stained-glass windows has been practiced for centuries. Some of the most exquisite examples are to be seen in medieval cathedrals in Europe. Stained-glass pictures are made up of pieces of colored glass, mounted in a lead framework. An artist paints details on the glass with colored enamels.

Glass is a ceramic product made not from clay, but from another common material – sand. To make glass, sand is heated in a furnace with a material called a flux, which helps the mixture melt. This happens at a temperature of about 1,500°C (2,700°F). When the molten mass cools and sets hard, it becomes transparent glass.

Ordinary window glass is called soda-lime glass because it is made using a flux of soda ash and lime. These are roasted forms of sodium carbonate and limestone. The heavier and more sparkling glass called lead crystal contains lead oxide. Colored glasses contain oxides of copper, chromium, and other metals.

Refractories

These are substances with exceptional resistance to heat. They are used, for example, to line furnaces and to make pots, or crucibles, for melting metals. Refractory materials include aluminum oxide, pure silica (the same mineral as sand), and graphite, a natural form of carbon. Synthetic refractories include tungsten carbide and boron nitride. Tungsten carbide is widely used to make bits for drilling. These bits are able to run red-hot without softening.

◄ Putting ceramic tiles on the space shuttle orbiter. The tiles form the heat shield for the craft, protecting it from frictional heating during reentry into the atmosphere. Something like 30,000 tiles are on the orbiter, held by adhesive. They are made of pure silica fiber and have the most remarkable insulating properties. They can be red-hot outside but cool enough inside to be touched by the bare hand.

Synthetics

Many of the products we use today are made from manufactured materials, rather than natural materials. They are artificial, or synthetic. Some, such as synthetic rubber, are designed to imitate materials which occur in nature. Others, such as nylon and polyvinyl chloride, have no natural counterpart.

Plastics are by far the commonest group of synthetic materials we use. They now rank alongside iron, wood, and concrete as the most important materials of our age. Plastics are made mainly from petrochemicals: chemicals obtained by refining oil, or petroleum. Petrochemicals are also the starting point for many other products, including drugs, dyes, paints, and insecticides.

▶ Plastics, the most widespread synthetics, are popular materials for making toys. They can take a lot of knocks without breaking. They keep their color, because the plastic is colored all the way through. No harm comes to children who chew them, because they are nontoxic.

The pioneers

The first successful plastic was made in 1870 by the American inventor John W. Hyatt. He was searching for a substitute for ivory to make billiard balls. The plastic he invented was celluloid. He made it by treating the cellulose in wood with nitric and sulfuric acids. This produced nitrocellulose, a material that by itself is too brittle to be useful. Hyatt made it into a useful product by adding a little camphor to it. This made it flexible.

Celluloid is not a completely synthetic material. Its starting point is a natural material, cellulose, which is then processed. It was not until 1909 that an American chemist, Leo H. Baekeland, produced the first fully synthetic plastic, which he made wholly from chemicals. He called it Bakelite.

Baekeland was at the time carrying out experiments to find new materials for making varnishes. In his research he found that the chemicals phenol and formaldehyde reacted together to form a resinous substance. By controlling the reaction, Baekeland found he made a material that could be molded by heat. This discovery led to the birth of the plastics industry.

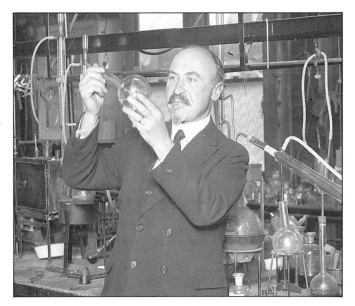

▲ The inventor of Bakelite, Leo H. Baekeland, at work in his laboratory. A chemist by profession, Baekeland was born in Belgium. He emigrated to the United States in 1889, at the age of 26.

▼ These desktop items made from Bakelite date from the 1940s. Bakelite became widely available in the 1920s. In the early days it was often used, as here, for making luxury goods.

Refining the crude

When Baekeland made the first completely synthetic plastic, Bakelite, one of the raw materials was phenol – from coal tar, then the most important source of raw materials for the newly emerging organic chemical industry.

Coal tar was then produced on a large scale as a by-product in the manufacture of coal gas. It contained a mixture of hydrocarbons, compounds of carbon and hydrogen only. From these compounds, chemists began to make dyes such as mauve, and drugs such as aspirin. They made explosives such as TNT, and eventually plastics such as nylon.

By the 1930s demand for organic chemicals had outstripped the supplies available from coal tar. Producers gradually switched to petroleum as a source instead. Today it is the major source.

Petroleum, or crude oil, is a thick greenish black liquid, made up almost entirely of liquid hydrocarbons. It contains literally thousands of them. But it becomes useful only when it is split up into different parts, or fractions, containing hydrocarbons having a similar boiling point.

The splitting up is done by distillation, also called fractionation. This process is a standard method for separating liquids with different boiling points. First the crude oil is heated in a

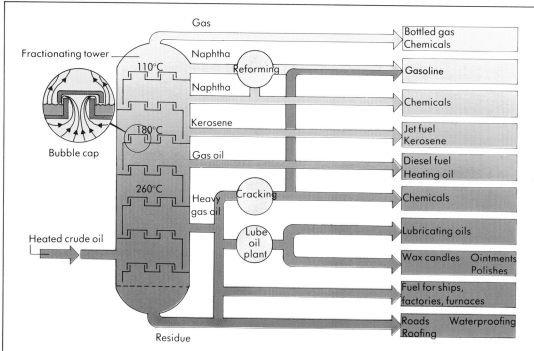

Fractionation

Crude oil is split up into its fractions in a fractionating tower. The hydrocarbons in oil vapor separate out at different levels according to their boiling point. Some hydrocarbon mixtures, such as gasoline, can be used more or less as they come from the tower. But most undergo further processing to make them into more desirable products. Some are transformed into chemical raw materials.

furnace to a temperature of about 400°C (750°F), whereupon much of it turns to vapor. The hot liquid and vapor is then fed into a fractionating tower up to 80 m (260 ft.) high.

Inside, the tower has about 40 perforated trays fixed at different levels across it. Each tray contains liquid hydrocarbons kept at a certain temperature. Temperatures decrease going up the column. Vapor rising up the tower passes through so-called bubble caps, which make it bubble through the liquid in each tray. Each hydrocarbon condenses out of the vapor as it bubbles through the tray kept at a temperature just below its own boiling point.

Many of the fractions obtained by distillation go for further processing. The hydrocarbons they contain are chemically altered to make them into more useful products. Some processes aim to increase the yield of gasoline. Others aim to produce raw materials for the organic chemical industry, called petrochemicals.

▲ Lit up at night, an oil refinery has a strange beauty. It is a huge chemical plant, covering several hundred hectares. The tallest structures are fractionating towers.

▼ Examples of the hydrocarbons found in crude oil. Hexane is a straight-chain compound. Cyclohexane and benzene are ring compounds, with single and double bonds, respectively, between their six carbon atoms.

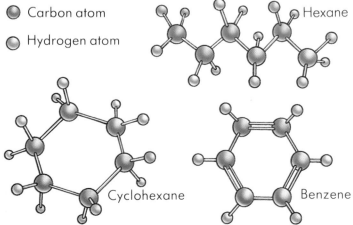

Carbon atom

Hydrogen atom

Hexane

Cyclohexane

Benzene

Petrochemicals

The main purpose of petroleum refining has always been to produce fuels, particularly gasoline. The initial fractionation of crude oil, however, yields only about one-third gasoline, which is the lightest fraction of distillation and the one with the lowest boiling point. Beginning in the 1920s, new methods were developed to improve the gasoline yield by processing heavier fractions. These processes are cracking and polymerization.

Breaking down
The most important cracking method requires the use of a catalyst, and is known as catalytic cracking. The object of the cracking operation is to "crack," or split up, larger, heavier hydrocarbon molecules into smaller, lighter ones.

The raw material, or feedstock, for cracking is usually the heavy gas oil fraction from the fractionating tower. It is fed into a vessel called a reactor, which is kept at a temperature of about 490°C (over 900°F) and at a pressure of two atmospheres (twice normal atmospheric pressure). Inside the reactor, a flow of vapor and air keeps the particles of catalyst suspended in a fluidlike, or fluidized, state. This allows intimate mixing of catalyst and vapor and provides ideal conditions for cracking.

The cracked oil vapor is led off to a fractionating tower. From there it goes to other units, which separate out the newly formed lighter hydrocarbons. The most valuable products are naphtha and gases. The naphtha is blended with the gasoline fraction.

Building up, rearranging
The gases consist of hydrocarbons with small molecules and a low boiling point which are of no use for fuel. So they are now fed to the polymerization unit, which builds up the small molecules into bigger ones, the opposite of cracking.

Polymerization takes place at a relatively low temperature (200°C, about 400°F), but at a very high pressure, nearly 70 times normal atmospheric pressure. The result is more hydrocarbons suitable for gasoline and others suitable as chemical raw materials.

Another refinery process, called reforming, also improves the gasoline yield. It does not

▼ Petroleum is a vast storehouse of chemical raw materials that has accumulated in the ground over 200 million years or more. Burning petroleum as a fuel in engines and furnaces seems a shameful waste of such a precious asset. The diagram gives an idea of how versatile petroleum is as a raw material. All these things can be made from two tanks full of gasoline, which would take a car about 1,000 km (over 600 mi.).

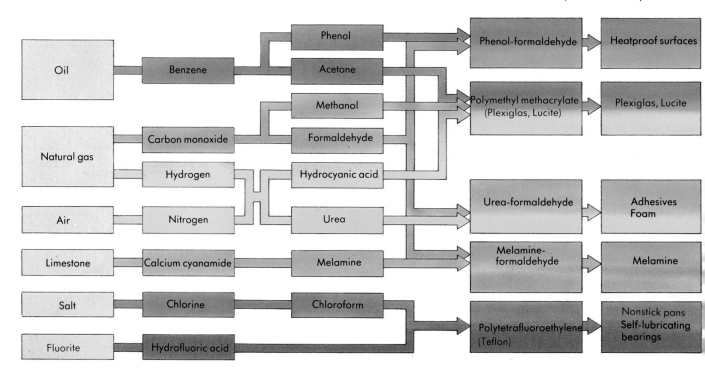

break down or build up molecules like the other processes. Rather it rearranges the atoms in the molecules. Reforming is a high-temperature, high-pressure process that requires a catalyst. It uses naphtha as a feedstock and produces a high proportion of "aromatics," or benzene compounds. These improve the burning qualities of gasoline. Alternatively, the reformed naphtha is available as a source of benzene and other aromatics for the chemical industry.

Petroleum chemicals

Catalytic cracking and reforming are two major refinery processes that produce chemicals as by-products. So does another – steam cracking. Naphtha and gas oil are the main feedstocks for this process. It takes place at a temperature of about 770°C (1,400°F) and at atmospheric pressure. Steam is mixed with the feedstock before it enters the cracking furnace.

Steam cracking yields liquids rich in aromatics suitable for gasoline. But the most important products are substances called alkenes (or olefins). These are unsaturated hydrocarbons, which means that they contain double or triple bonds between some of their carbon atoms. These double bonds can be easily broken in chemical reactions. In other words, unsaturated hydrocarbons are highly reactive.

By far the most important alkene is ethylene (ethene). It has the chemical formula C_2H_4 or $H_2C=CH_2$, where = means a double bond. The best-known use of ethylene is for making the plastic polyethylene (polyethene) by polymerization. The plastic polyvinyl chloride is made by polymerizing vinyl chloride, a chlorine compound of ethylene.

Steam cracking also yields large quantities of propylene (propene), much of which is made into polypropylene and other plastics. Butadiene, another product, is made into synthetic rubber in combination with styrene.

▼ This diagram shows how chemists fashion a host of synthetic products from a mix of raw materials. These materials are derived not only from petroleum, but also from a variety of other sources as well. These sources include air and natural gas, which is a mixture of light hydrocarbon gases, mainly methane. Limestone (calcium carbonate), salt (sodium chloride), and fluorite (calcium fluoride) are mineral raw materials.

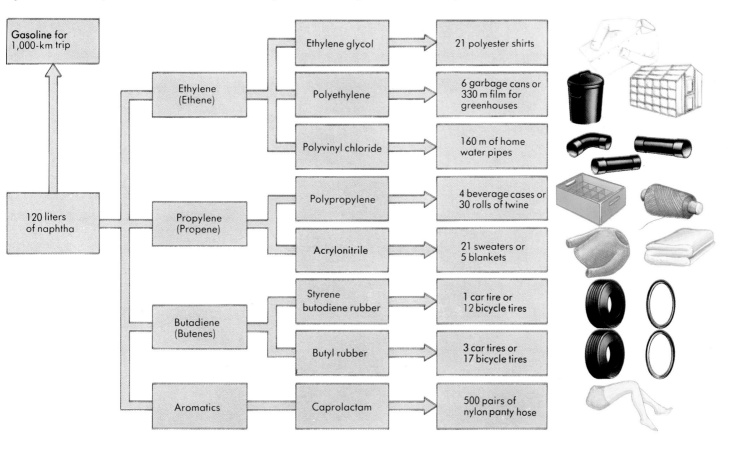

Composites

▲ Many sailboats have their hulls made of fiberglass. Unlike wood, the traditional material for boat hulls, fiberglass resists rotting and is tough enough to resist knocks.

The best pole-vaulters can clear heights of up to 6 m (over 19 ft.). To achieve such lofty heights, they need to use a pole made from a synthetic material, so flexible that it can bend almost double. This material is fiberglass. It is the most familiar example of a kind of material we call a composite.

Composites are made of a substance, usually plastic, in which fibers are embedded. The fibers reinforce the plastic, and give it extra strength. They tend to stop it from cracking when it is put under stress. As well as glass, a number of other kinds of fibers are used in composites, including those made from carbon, refractory materials, and metals.

In devising this method of reinforcing with fibers, scientists are copying nature. One of the most remarkable structural materials in nature, bone, is a composite. It is made up of the mineral calcium phosphate, reinforced with fibers of a protein called collagen. This combination makes bone light but very strong.

Fiberglass-reinforced plastics

The correct name for the fiberglass material is fiberglass-reinforced plastic (FRP). Glass fibers may be made in long lengths, or filaments, by melting glass and forcing it through a spinneret. This is a device perforated with hundreds of holes. Alternatively, fibers can be produced in the form of "wool" using a rotating perforated drum. Molten glass introduced into the drum is flung out through the holes by centrifugal force, forming fibers which then break up into short lengths.

Typical FRP products include boat hulls, car bodies, and luggage. These are made by a molding process. First a mold is made of the required object. Then a mat of glass fibers is laid over it. A synthetic resin (usually polyester) is then poured over the mat. It is mixed with a curing agent, which makes it set into hard plastic. Alternatively, for some products, the glass fiber is chopped very finely and mixed with the resin. This mixture is then sprayed over the mold with a spray gun.

Carbon fibers

Plastics reinforced with carbon fiber have the desirable properties of lightness coupled with strength. They are used in aircraft construction, for example, to make wing and body sections; in medicine to make artificial limbs; and to make sports equipment.

Carbon is unique among the chemical elements in being able to bond strongly with itself to form huge molecules. Most synthetic plastics have such molecules. They are formed of long chains of carbon atoms, to which are attached other atoms (such as hydrogen) or groups of atoms.

Carbon fibers are made by baking plastic fibers, such as acrylics, in an oven. By carefully controlling this process, the side atoms on the molecules can be removed, leaving the very strong long carbon chains. The fibers produced have exceptional stiffness and, weight for weight, have four times the strength of steel.

Fibers similar to carbon fibers can be made from the element boron. But unlike carbon fibers, boron fibers are electrical insulators.

Laminates and cermets

In a broader sense, composites also include a variety of other synthetic construction materials. They include, for example, plastic laminates. The heatproof working surfaces in kitchens are laminates of synthetic resins, reinforced with paper or cloth.

Cermets are combinations of ceramics and metals, for example, aluminum oxide and chromium. They are designed to combine the heat resistance of ceramics with the strength and machinability of metals. They are widely used for making components for the high-temperature parts of jet and rocket engines.

▼ In making a helicopter blade from FRP, glass fibers have been wound around a mold. Liquid resin will next be applied, which will set into plastic.

▼ A pole-vaulter accelerates as he runs up to the bar. The fiberglass pole he carries is flexible. It will bend and then spring back to help propel him high into the air.

Part Two

Manufacturing

The word manufacturing literally means "making by hand." But the vast majority of the products we use, from ball bearings and bottles to carpets and cars, are manufactured by machines in factories.

Machines hold the key to modern manufacturing, particularly machines controlled by computers. Computers are changing our industries, patterns of employment, and way of life very rapidly. These changes may be as great as in the Industrial Revolution beginning in the 1700s.

This part of the book outlines how major branches of the manufacturing industry transform materials into finished products. It covers metalworking techniques, such as forging and welding; chemical technologies, such as acid and plastics manufacture, food processing, the synthesizing of drugs, and papermaking; spinning and weaving; and production of the silicon chip.

◄ Imported cars from Japan. Advances in steelmaking have made cars inexpensive enough for many to own them. The automobile industry pioneered the use of assembly lines.

Production

Spot facts

• The introduction of the Bessemer steelmaking process in 1856 reduced the cost of steel by more than 90 percent, to about $12 a ton.

• The introduction of automation in some heavy industries, such as steelmaking, has reduced the workforce by up to 90 percent.

• The introduction of computers and word processors in business, which was supposed to bring about the "paperless office," has in fact led to a marked increase in world paper consumption.

Most of our goods are made or processed in factories by machines. Machines were first introduced on a wide scale during the Industrial Revolution, which began in Great Britain in the early 1700s and spread gradually to the rest of the world. It did more than change industry. It also changed people's lives. People flocked from the land into cities to work in factories. What had been a rural society started to become an industrial one.

The use of machines in factories and the careful organization of labor are still the key factors in manufacturing today. They allow the efficient mass production of goods at low cost.

► An operator at the control panel of an automated steel-rolling mill. In the mill a red-hot slab of steel passes at ever-increasing speed between sets of heavy rollers. The control computer automatically sets the gap between each set of rollers according to the temperature and thickness of the steel coming from the previous set of rollers.

The Industrial Revolution

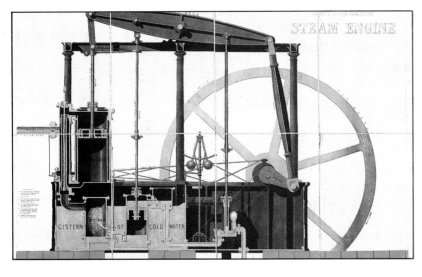

STEAM ENGINE

CISTERN OF COLD WATER

◀ James Watt's double-acting steam engine of the 1780s, the machine that powered the Industrial Revolution. Steam was introduced to each side of the piston in turn, making each piston stroke (movement) a power stroke. With its separate condenser, it was four times more powerful than Thomas Newcomen's engine of the early 1700s.

▼ Four milestones in the development of industry. The spinning jenny helped transform textile making into an industry. The screw-cutting lathe was one of the first precision machine tools. The *Rocket* locomotive ushered in a revolution in transportation; the Bessemer process, a revolution in steelmaking.

The Industrial Revolution began in textile making. This ancient craft was transformed in Great Britain from a domestic activity into an industry by a series of inventions in spinning and weaving. In 1733 John Kay invented a mechanical shuttle, which greatly speeded up weaving. This created an increased demand for spun yarn. And so others developed machines to spin yarn faster: James Hargreaves, with the spinning jenny (1767); Richard Arkwright, with the water frame (1769); and Samuel Crompton, with the spinning mule (1779).

Now the looms could not cope with the extra yarn, and so Edmund Cartwright built a steam-powered loom (1785) to speed weaving. With speedier spinning and weaving, the cotton growers in the United States could no longer supply cotton fast enough. But in 1792 an American, Eli Whitney, speeded up the slowest part of cotton production – separating the fibers from the seeds. His cotton gin could separate the fibers 50 times faster than by hand.

The application of steam power to industry began first in coal mining in the early 1700s in England. First Thomas Savery and then Thomas Newcomen devised steam pumping machines. But it took the genius of James Watt to convert the steam engine into a reliable and compact power source. The success of Watt's engine in turn depended on John Wilkinson's invention (1775) of a machine for boring the engine cylinder accurately. And so it went, with each invention playing its part in a revolution that has continued to the present day.

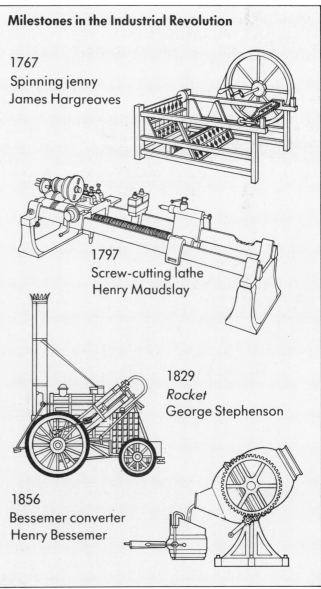

Milestones in the Industrial Revolution

1767
Spinning jenny
James Hargreaves

1797
Screw-cutting lathe
Henry Maudslay

1829
Rocket
George Stephenson

1856
Bessemer converter
Henry Bessemer

The factory

▶ Richard Arkwright invented this roller-spinning machine in 1769. On the machine a loose "rope" of fibers was drawn out into fine yarn by sets of rotating rollers. Then the yarn was twisted by a rotating "flyer" as it was wound on to a bobbin. The machine was driven by a moving belt from a waterwheel and was known as a water frame.

Richard Arkwright invented the water frame spinning machine, but that was not all. In 1771 he installed a large number of water frames in a building at Cromford, in Derbyshire, England. He employed people to operate them, thus pioneering the factory system.

Cloth is an example of a product that is made directly from raw materials. Many other goods are produced by assembling, or putting together, sets of ready-made components that are nearly identical. This method was pioneered in the late 1700s by Eli Whitney.

In 1798 Whitney contracted to produce 10,000 muskets for the U.S. army in two years. This was a tall order because even a highly skilled gunsmith could make only a few guns in a year. He would make all the parts himself and tailor them to fit together. Each musket would be slightly different. Whitney tackled the problem another way. First he designed machines that could turn out near-identical parts each time. He employed skilled engineers for this part of the operation. Then he employed unskilled people to assemble the muskets from sets of parts. In this venture Whitney also established another manufacturing principle: the use of precision machine tools to create near-identical, or interchangeable parts, which can then be put together by semiskilled labor.

The American automobile maker Henry Ford established another manufacturing principle in 1913. That year he introduced the moving assembly line into his factory making the famous "Model T" Ford. In this method of assembly, workers were positioned at some 50 points next to a track, along which moved the car frame. As the frame moved past, each worker would attach a part to it until, at the end of the line, the car was complete. Since each worker had to perform only one task, it could be done very quickly indeed.

The latest chapter in the factory story features computers. Machines, machine tools, and even whole production networks are being brought under computer control. This leads to automation, a system in which machines regulate themselves. Modern factories incorporate some or all of these features – machines, precision machine tools, interchangeable parts, moving assembly lines, and automatic computer control.

◀ The production line in an automated factory making Macintosh computers. No human workers are to be seen. The few workers there are in the factory are present to oversee operations. Computer-manufacture hinges on the production of silicon chips and electronic circuits, which can be designed and checked only by other computers.

▶ A robot welder at work. Robot welding machines are now common in manufacturing. They work accurately and are unaffected by heat, glare, and fumes. A camera sends pictures of the exact position of the workpiece to the robot, which adjusts its arm in order to make the weld in the correct position.

Organization

The production of goods by machines in a factory is the visible aspect of manufacturing. But there are many other aspects, including design, sales, market research, finance, and labor relations. For example, the products being made must be of the right design and sell at the right price. Otherwise, nobody will buy them. Market research will often need to be carried out to find out from potential customers what are the right goods and the right price. Enough goods must be sold to pay for the cost of setting up production, paying for raw materials, paying the work force, and so on. The workers must be paid a reasonable wage for what they do and be given reasonable working conditions. Otherwise, they will become discontented, disputes will break out, and production will be lost.

For a manufacturing operation to work

▶ Picking grapes for wine making in the Loire region of France. Many of the small French wine producers have formed cooperatives. These are loose companies in which members share wine-making equipment and marketing facilities, yet still remain largely independent.

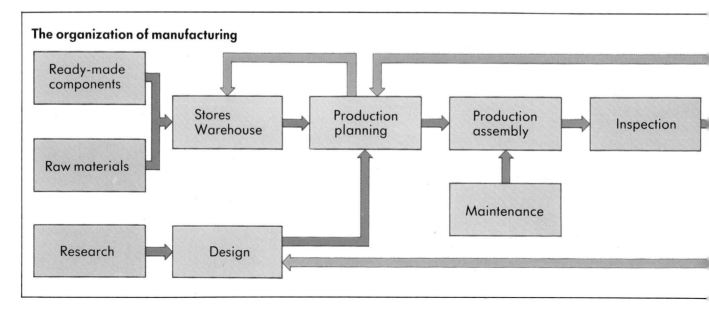

The organization of manufacturing

successfully, it must be well organized in every aspect. The kind of organization needed varies widely according to the size and nature of the operation. In a small company, which employs only a handful of people, the owner takes responsibility for everything, from design to marketing and employee relations.

The management

In a large company, reponsibilities are shared by a team of managers. There may be several senior managers, each responsible for the operation and organization of a department which deals with one aspect of the manufacturing operation, such as production, sales, or marketing. These executives have staff under them, who carry out their instructions. The executives carry out policies laid down by the owner or a board of directors.

A corporation has a board of directors, who are answerable to stockholders. These are people who have invested money in the company by buying stock. Their money provides working capital for the company, enabling it to develop new processes and new products. The company pays the stockholders a dividend, or percentage of any profit it makes.

Producing the goods

The initial idea for a new product may come from a variety of sources. For example, the sales team may spot a gap in the market. Or company scientists may make a brilliant discovery. The idea is taken up by the design and research departments, which look at the possible new product from every viewpoint. For example, they may experiment with different kinds of materials to find the one most suitable, and they will investigate methods of production. They may build mock-ups, or full-size models, of the product, and maybe one or more prototypes, or examples of the finished product.

If the new project is given the go-ahead, production planners draw up detailed plans for manufacturing. They work out what raw materials, tools, machines, and workers are required to produce the goods in the numbers required. And they draw up schedules and flowcharts to ensure that the right materials, tools, machines, and workers are always in the right place at the right time in the process.

The manufacturing process will involve the production of components from raw materials, or the assembly of components into a finished product, or both. Machining operations by machine tools will often be involved. After manufacture, the goods will be inspected and periodically tested. Any substandard ones will be rejected. This is called quality control. The goods are finally packaged ready for distribution to retailers or wholesalers. Retailers sell the goods to the public; wholesalers sell to retailers. Sometimes the goods may be sold directly to customers by the sales team.

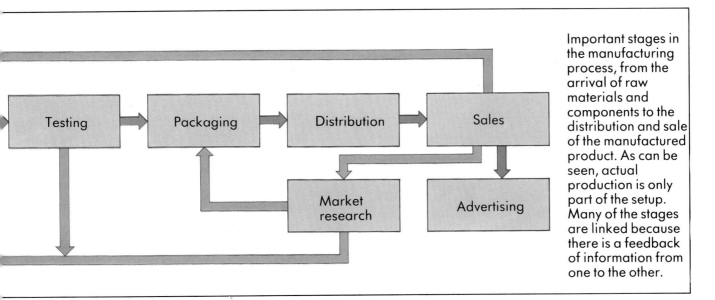

Important stages in the manufacturing process, from the arrival of raw materials and components to the distribution and sale of the manufactured product. As can be seen, actual production is only part of the setup. Many of the stages are linked because there is a feedback of information from one to the other.

Working with metals

Most of the metals we use are produced by smelting ores at high temperatures in furnaces. They leave the furnace in a molten state. They then have to be processed into finished products. The shaping process selected depends on the metal concerned and what it is to be used for. A metal may be shaped when it is molten, when red-hot, or when cold. It may be molded, rolled, hammered, squeezed, or welded. Afterward it may be turned, ground, drilled, or milled to very precise dimensions by machine tools. Precision machining holds the key to most manufacturing processes.

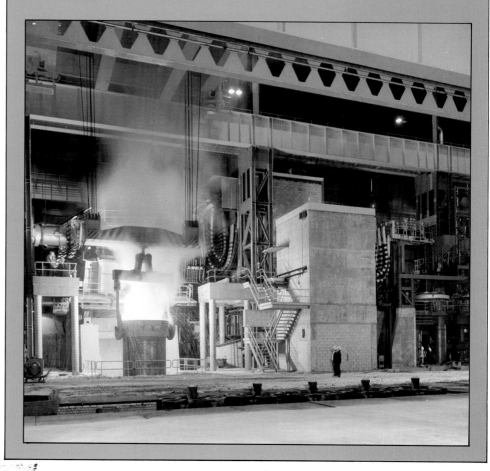

► White-hot steel pours into a traveling ladle from an electric-arc furnace. Next it will be cast into molds, where it will solidify into ingots. These will then go to other machines for final shaping.

Casting

The technique of shaping metals by casting has been practiced for at least 6,000 years. Casting is a process in which molten metal is poured into shaped molds and allowed to cool. As it cools, it sets, or becomes solid, and takes the shape of the mold. Copper and bronze were the first metals shaped by casting because they could be melted in the early furnaces. Bronze is still widely used for casting, to make such things as statues and ship propellers. The most common casting metal, however, is iron. Machinery bodies such as engine blocks are cast in iron, because cast iron is hard and rigid.

Sand casting

Casting takes place in a foundry. The most common method is sand casting. A model of the object to be made is placed in a box and a moist sand and clay mixture is packed tightly around it. A cavity of the required shape remains when the model is removed. Usually the mold is made in two halves to allow the model to be removed. Two holes are made in the top of the mold. The metal is poured in through one (called the runner), while the other (the riser) allows the air to escape from inside. The mold is broken open to release the casting when cool.

In a variation of this process, the model is made in wax. After the mold has been made, it is heated and the wax is poured out. Molten metal is then poured in. This method is called investment casting or the lost-wax (*cire perdue*) process. It is often used by artists, and to make precision castings for engines.

Die-casting

This is a method of casting that takes place in a metal mold, or die, into which molten metal is forced. The mold can be reused.

In what is called permanent-mold casting, molten metal is simply poured into a mold. This is used to make simple shapes such as pipes.

Die-casting can produce more intricate shapes – by injecting molten metal into a water-cooled mold under pressure. This method is widely used to make parts for machines and appliances. Alloys containing zinc, tin, aluminum, and magnesium are favored because they have a low melting point. Die-casting is very suitable for mass production.

▲ Workers handling a still red-hot casting of a railroad car wheel, which has just been removed from its mold. It is cast in steel.

Sand casting

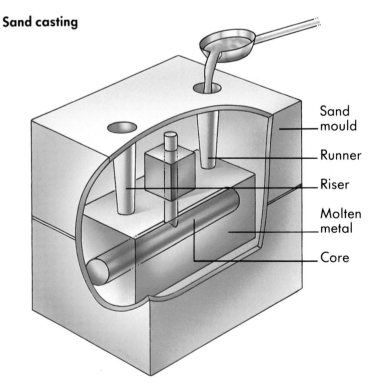

Sand mould

Runner

Riser

Molten metal

Core

▲ The principle of sand casting. Molten metal is poured into a hollow mold, which has the shape of the object to be made. To produce a hollow object, a core must be included. The metal is poured into the mold until it fills both the runner and the riser.

Rolling

Rolling is a process in which metal is passed between heavy rotating rollers, rather like clothes through an old-fashioned wringer. In a rolling mill the metal is passed through a succession of rollers, each pair being slightly closer together than those before. In this way the metal is squeezed thinner and thinner. Mostly, metal is rolled when it is red-hot. In this state it can "flow" more easily.

Much of the metal produced in furnaces is first cast into ingots. Usually these are then reduced to a more convenient size by rolling. The metal emerges as a flat slab, which may then go for shaping by another method, such as forging. Or it may be rolled further, for example, in a continuous strip mill. This produces coils of thin sheet, or strip. The slab goes slowly into the first set of rollers, but comes from the last set traveling at a speed of up to 100 km/h (60 mph or more). The hot-rolled strip is then usually rolled again when cold. Cold rolling improves the finish and hardness.

▲ Steel strip coming off a cold-rolling mill. During cold rolling the metal becomes brittle, which could cause it to crack in use. It therefore undergoes a heat treatment called annealing to bring it back to a reasonable condition. It is first heated and then it is allowed to cool slowly.

◄ High above the city streets, workers piece together a frame of steel girders that will support a new tower block. The girders are shaped with a typical H cross section in rolling mills, using rollers with grooves cut in them.

Forging

Forging shapes metal by hammering or pressing. It is the oldest shaping method. In early times metals were hammered by hand, much as a traditional blacksmith does today. But in industry today forging is done by machine.

In a drop forge, a hammering action is produced by a falling hammer, or ram. The ram is raised again by air or steam pressure. Air or steam pressure may also be used to help accelerate the ram downward to deliver an even more powerful blow. The ram shapes the metal by forcing it into a mold, or die.

Usually the ram carries the upper part of the die, while the lower part is mounted on the forge bed. The metal blank, usually hot, is placed on the lower die, and the ram is released. The metal is forced into shape as the two halves of the die come together. Stamping is a kind of small-scale drop-forging process used to make coins and medals.

On a forging press metal is forced into shape not by a hammer blow, but by a gradual squeezing action. The press works by hydraulic (liquid) pressure. Some presses can exert a force of up to 50,000 metric tons. They are used, for example, to shape massive red-hot steel ingots. Smaller hydraulic presses are used to shape car body panels from cold steel sheet.

▲ A blacksmith practises the traditional craft of forging. A strip of metal is heated up in the forge fire, and then hammered into shape on an anvil. The metal is cooled by plunging it into cold water.

◄ Forging the rotor shaft of a turbine on a massive forging press. The shaft is beginning to take shape. It started off as an ingot casting, which was reheated until it was red-hot. Then it was placed on the press and slowly squeezed into shape under a pressure of thousands of tons exerted by the hydraulic ram. Later, it will be machined on a lathe to bring it to the dimensions required in a rotor shaft.

Joining metals

Riveting

Many metal objects are so large or so complicated that they cannot be produced in one piece, but must be built up little by little. A ship's hull is an example. Until about the middle of the century, most hulls were built of steel plates joined together by rivets. A rivet is a metal plug with a rounded head at one end.

In riveting, holes are drilled in overlapping plates. Rivets are inserted through them and hammered to form a second head. The metal plates are then sandwiched tightly together. Riveting is no longer much used for producing ships' hulls, although it is still widely used elsewhere in shipbuilding. It is also used in aircraft construction for building the airframe and the outer "skin" of the fuselage and wings.

Welding

Most ships' hulls these days are constructed of steel plates that are welded together. The plates are joined edge to edge, with no overlap, which saves weight and materials.

In welding, the edges of the metal pieces to be joined are brought into contact and heated until they begin to melt and merge, or fuse together.

▶ A welder joins together two lengths of pipeline for the North Sea oil fields. The method is electric welding, using a special circular electrode. The welder wears thick protective clothing and a head mask as protection against the shower of sparks and glare which the welding process generates.

▼ These are the two main methods of producing a strong joint between pieces of metal. In riveting, headed rivets clamp overlapping metal plates together. In welding, joints are produced when touching pieces of metal melt and fuse together. Welded joints can be of different types, which include butt, lap, fillet, and spot welds.

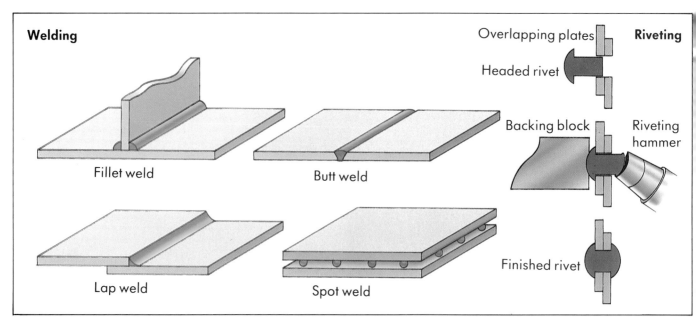

Welding

Fillet weld

Butt weld

Lap weld

Spot weld

Overlapping plates   Riveting

Headed rivet

Backing block   Riveting hammer

Finished rivet

Extra molten metal is often added from a so-called filler rod. When the metal in the joint cools, it forms a continuous structure linking the two pieces. The result is a strong joint.

There are three main methods of welding – gas, arc, and resistance welding. In gas welding the heat to melt the metal pieces and filler rod is provided by an oxyacetylene torch. The torch is so called because it burns acetylene gas with oxygen, at a temperature approaching 3,000°C (5,400°F). Arc welding, on the other hand, uses an electric arc – a kind of continuous spark – to produce a high temperature. The arc is struck by passing a heavy electric current between the metal to be joined and an electrode.

In resistance welding two electrodes carrying heavy current pinch together two overlapping plates. The resistance to the passage of electricity between the two electrodes produces enough heat to fuse the metal in between. This creates a spot weld. When a wheel or roller electrode is used, a continuous seam weld is formed.

Brazing and soldering are alternative methods of joining metals. They involve melting a noniron metal that has a lower melting point than the metals being joined.

▲ The former transatlantic liner *Queen Mary*, launched in 1934, is now a floating hotel and conference center at Long Beach, near Los Angeles. Like most ships of its day, the vessel, which is 310.8 m (1,020 ft.) long, is built of riveted steel plates.

▶ The huge Magnus oil-production rig just after construction. It was built by welding together sections of steel pipe, which measured 13 km (8 mi.) long overall and weighed 14,000 metric tons. It is now sited off the Shetland Islands of Great Britain.

Machining

Most metal objects shaped by casting, forging, or other methods need some kind of finishing treatment before they are ready for use. For example, they may need to have holes drilled or metal removed to bring them to the right size and shape. The machines that carry out such metal-finishing processes are known as machine tools. They play an important part in the modern assembly-line method of manufacturing because they can work to very accurate limits and produce near-identical parts.

Since machine tools are used to cut metal, they have powerful motors to drive the cutting tools. These tools are made from very hard tool steels, which retain their sharpness during machining. Special high-speed steels contain-

ing tungsten and chromium remain sharp even when they run red-hot. To help reduce temperatures during machining, the tool and workpiece are cooled by a light "cutting oil". This also helps lubricate the cutting operation.

The lathe

One of the most common machine tools in workshops is the lathe, on which a process called turning is carried out. On a lathe, a workpiece is rotated and various cutting tools are then moved in to cut it. The workpiece is rotated between a headstock at one end and a tailstock at the other. It is clamped in a chuck in the headstock, which also houses the motor that drives the chuck. A transmission allows the

▲ Machinists examine a wing panel for an Airbus plane, which is being cut to shape on a huge milling machine. Twin cutting heads are working on two panels. The wing panels on the plane are machined from solid metal. This method of construction is much stronger than conventional riveting.

▲ A lathe operator checks the diameter of a large turbine rotor with a gauge. The rotor was originally shaped on a hydraulic forging press. It is now being "turned" on a lathe, where metal will be removed until it is the right size. The chuck of the lathe is at the top; the tailstock is at the bottom.

workpiece to be driven at a number of speeds from, say, 20 to 2,000 revolutions per minute.

The cutting tools are mounted on a cross slide, which in turn is mounted on a saddle. The saddle moves lengthwise along the lathe, while the cross slide moves at right angles to it, so as to carry the tools toward or away from the rotating workpiece. The cross slide and the saddle both run on precision screw threads so that they can be positioned with great accuracy.

Drilling and milling

Another common machine tool is the drill press, which is used to drill holes. The workpiece is held stationary, while a rotating drill bit is lowered into it. The drill bit has cutting edges just at the tip and spiral grooves, or flutes, along the side. This allows the cut metal, known as swarf, to escape. Turret drills have a drill head that carries a number of drill bits of different sizes.

Milling is a machining operation carried out with a rotating toothed cutting wheel. Metal is removed as the workpiece moves past the wheel, which may rotate at speeds approaching 10,000 revolutions per minute.

Other machine tools carry out other metal-finishing operations. For example, a shaping machine uses a chisel-like tool to cut flat surfaces; a grinding machine uses a rotating abrasive wheel or a moving abrasive belt to remove metal.

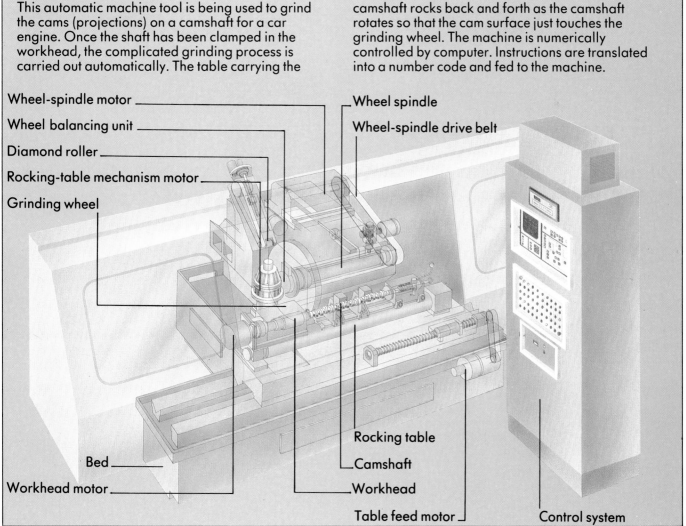

Automatic grinding machine

This automatic machine tool is being used to grind the cams (projections) on a camshaft for a car engine. Once the shaft has been clamped in the workhead, the complicated grinding process is carried out automatically. The table carrying the camshaft rocks back and forth as the camshaft rotates so that the cam surface just touches the grinding wheel. The machine is numerically controlled by computer. Instructions are translated into a number code and fed to the machine.

Wheel-spindle motor

Wheel balancing unit

Diamond roller

Rocking-table mechanism motor

Grinding wheel

Wheel spindle

Wheel-spindle drive belt

Bed

Workhead motor

Rocking table

Camshaft

Workhead

Table feed motor

Control system

The chemical industry

Spot facts

- The two most widely used industrial chemicals are sulfuric acid and ammonia.

- A large chemical plant producing caustic soda by the electrolysis of salt water uses as much electricity as a town of 300,000 people.

- Chemists have synthesized as many as 60,000 different kinds of plastics.

- Polyethylene plastic is made up of molecules that have up to 20,000 carbon atoms linked together in a long chain.

- A pair of nylon stockings is made up of more than 6 km (3¾ mi.) of yarn knitted into three million loops.

▶ A chemical engineer adjusts a valve regulating the flow of materials through a pilot plant. This is a small-scale chemical plant used for testing a new process. If it performs satisfactorily, a full-scale plant might be built.

From its beginnings in the 1700s, the chemical industry has grown into one of the largest industries there is. Its products, chemicals, are used in practically every other industry, from electronics to steelmaking. They are used in agriculture, for fertilizers and pesticides, and in the home, in paints, washing powders, hair sprays, and medicines. And most of us use, wear, and even eat the products made from, or processed with, chemicals. These range from margarine and paper to drip-dry shirts and nonstick cookware.

The chemical industry uses processes devised in the chemistry laboratory. It transforms raw materials into finished chemical products, or else into intermediate chemicals that other manufacturers turn into products.

Chemical engineering

Chemical engineering is the branch of engineering which designs, builds, and operates chemical plants, the factories in which chemicals are produced or processed.

Chemical engineers take a process from the chemistry laboratory and develop it on a large enough scale for industrial production. This is usually much more difficult than it sounds. For example, in the laboratory, heating a few milliliters of acid in a glass flask over a Bunsen burner presents few problems. But heating up thousands of liters of acid in an industrial plant is quite a different matter.

Each chemical manufacturing process uses raw materials and converts them into finished products. In this way, each process is different. However, every process involves a certain number of standard chemical and physical operations. Chemical engineers design suitable equipment to carry out these operations economically. Where possible, they use standard, rather than specially designed, equipment to keep down the cost.

Standard chemical operations are known as unit processes. They include oxidation, chlorination, and hydrogenation, in which, respectively, oxygen, chlorine, and hydrogen combine with other substances. Another important unit process is polymerization, in which small molecules are built up into larger ones.

Standard physical operations are known as unit operations. Common ones include mixing, filtering, distillation, evaporation, and drying.

► A chemist works in a laboratory on a method of vacuum-processing materials. There is no guarantee that a large-scale plant would be able to repeat the process successfully or economically.

▼ The diagram shows a likely time scale for the nine main stages from the birth of an idea to the production of a salable product – often taking more than five years from start to finish. It could take another five years for the plant to pay for itself.

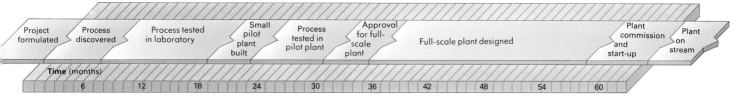

| Project formulated | Process discovered | Process tested in laboratory | Small pilot plant built | Process tested in pilot plant | Approval for full-scale plant | Full-scale plant designed | Plant commission and start-up | Plant on stream |

Time (months)

| 6 | 12 | 18 | 24 | 30 | 36 | 42 | 48 | 54 | 60 |

Heavy chemicals

The chemical industry produces vast tonnages of a wide range of chemicals. But a relatively small number of chemicals account for the bulk of production. These are generally called heavy chemicals, because they are produced in such large amounts. In contrast, some chemicals are produced only in small amounts. They are usually termed fine chemicals. They are also often the product of more complex chemical processing. Dyes and pharmaceuticals, or drugs, are examples of fine chemicals.

Most of the leading heavy chemicals are inorganic. They are made from salts, minerals, or gases in the air. Among the most important are sulfuric acid, ammonia, sodium hydroxide, and sodium carbonate. Sulfuric acid is vital to so many modern manufacturing processes that it is often called the "lifeblood of industry." But the other three chemicals mentioned are also vital to modern industry.

Early chemical industry
The modern chemical industry began in the 1790s. That is when Nicolas Leblanc, a French surgeon turned chemist, found a way of making sodium carbonate on an industrial scale. The chemical was much in demand for making soap and glass. The first stage of the Leblanc process was to treat sodium chloride (common salt) with sulfuric acid. The demand for sulfuric acid for the Leblanc process led in turn to an improved process for making the acid, called the lead-chamber process. This was later superseded by the present method, which is called the contact process.

Salt water is the starting point for the modern method of making sodium carbonate. This is called the ammonia-soda process because it involves a series of reactions with ammonia. Salt water is also the raw material for making caustic soda, or sodium hydroxide. But this time no lengthy series of chemical reactions is involved. Caustic soda is produced simply by passing an electric current through the salt water. This method, electrolysis, is a useful way of producing many metals and chemicals.

▶ This plant makes ammonia by combining nitrogen and hydrogen in the presence of an iron-oxide catalyst. The process, called the Haber process, takes place at about 400°C (750°F) and at a pressure of up to 1,000 atmospheres.

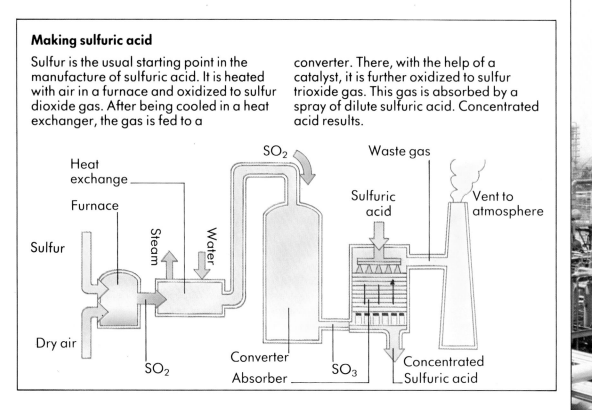

Making sulfuric acid

Sulfur is the usual starting point in the manufacture of sulfuric acid. It is heated with air in a furnace and oxidized to sulfur dioxide gas. After being cooled in a heat exchanger, the gas is fed to a converter. There, with the help of a catalyst, it is further oxidized to sulfur trioxide gas. This gas is absorbed by a spray of dilute sulfuric acid. Concentrated acid results.

Heat exchange
Furnace
Steam
Water
SO_2
Waste gas
Sulfuric acid
Vent to atmosphere
Sulfur
Dry air
SO_2
Converter
Absorber
SO_3
Concentrated Sulfuric acid

► The main uses of four of the world's leading industrial chemicals. A major use of sulfuric acid and ammonia is to make fertilizers. The acid is used to make superphosphate; ammonia is used to make ammonium nitrate and urea. Caustic soda, or sodium hydroxide, is used for making soap, paper, and artificial silks. One of sodium carbonate's most useful applications is in the manufacture of glass.

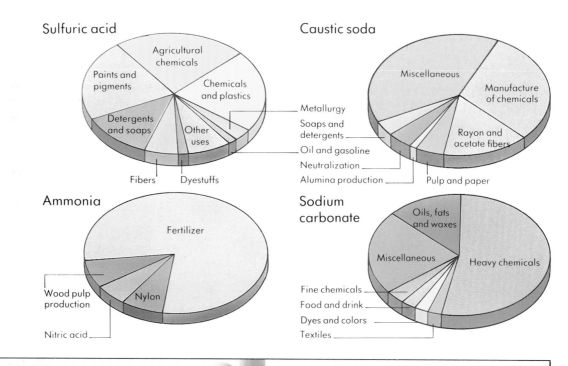

Sulfuric acid

Agricultural chemicals
Paints and pigments
Chemicals and plastics
Detergents and soaps
Other uses
Metallurgy
Fibers
Dyestuffs

Caustic soda

Miscellaneous
Manufacture of chemicals
Soaps and detergents
Rayon and acetate fibers
Oil and gasoline
Neutralization
Alumina production
Pulp and paper

Ammonia

Fertilizer
Wood pulp production
Nylon
Nitric acid

Sodium carbonate

Oils, fats and waxes
Miscellaneous
Heavy chemicals
Fine chemicals
Food and drink
Dyes and colors
Textiles

Plastics

Plastics are now close to metals in being the most important industrial products of our age. We can define a plastic as a substance which has a long-chain molecule, and which can be molded into shape when heated.

It is the long-chain molecules of plastics that make them so special. Most ordinary substances have short molecules, with just a few atoms linked together. Plastics, however, have long molecules containing thousands of atoms, almost always with a "backbone" of linked carbon atoms. Carbon is the only element that can link together in this way.

The raw materials for most plastics are hydrocarbons obtained from oil refining. The most useful of these is the gas ethylene (ethene). This has a short molecule with a backbone of just two carbon atoms. However, at high temperature and pressure, thousands of the short ethylene molecules will link together to form a long-chain molecule. We call ethylene a monomer ("one part"); the long-chain molecule, a polymer ("many parts"); and the process, polymerization. We know this particular polymer as polyethylene; it is also sometimes called polyethene.

Thousands of plastics can be produced by the polymerization of suitable hydrocarbons or their derivatives. Among other well-known plastics are polyvinyl chloride, nylon, polypropylene, and polystyrene. All these plastics will soften when reheated. They are known as thermosoftening plastics, or thermoplastics. The other main group of plastics set rigid when they are heat-molded into shape and will not soften when reheated. They are called thermosetting plastics, or thermosets. They include the original synthetic plastic, Bakelite (phenol-formaldehyde), and its relatives urea- and melamine-formaldehyde.

▲ Like other modern cars, this MGB Roadster uses many different kinds of plastics. The tires are made from synthetic rubber, as are the shock-absorbing bumpers. The paint was made using plastic resins, while the upholstery and carpets are woven from synthetic fibers. The hood is made from polyvinyl chloride, textured to imitate leather.

► A reservoir on Tenerife, Canary Islands, lined with polyvinyl chloride.

Synthetic rubber

Many products used today are made from synthetic rubbers. They are a kind of "elastic plastic," a material called an elastomer. The search for a substitute for rubber led German chemists to produce the first successful synthetic rubber in 1926. Called Buna rubber, it was made from butadiene, a chemical closely related to isoprene, the monomer in the sap of the rubber tree.

The most common synthetic rubber today is a copolymer (mixed polymer) of butadiene and styrene. Neoprene is a synthetic rubber made from acetylene (ethyne). It was one of the first to be discovered, by Wallace H. Carothers in 1931, and is still widely used because of its excellent resistance to high temperatures, oils, and chemicals.

Shaping plastics

By far the commonest methods of shaping plastics involve molding. Thermoplastics such as polyethylene and polyvinyl chloride are easy to mold into shapes, and various methods are possible. Bowls, for example, are made by injection molding. This involves heating the plastic until it is molten and then injecting it into a shaped, water-cooled mold.

Bottles and hollow toys can be made by blow molding. A blob of molten plastic is delivered into a hollow mold, and then air is blown into it through a pipe. The plastic is forced against the mold and takes its shape.

Thermosetting plastics, such as Bakelite, have to be shaped by a different technique, called compression molding. They cannot be shaped like thermoplastics because they melt and set more or less at the same time. During their manufacture, the polymerization process is halted before the molecules begin to cross-link and set hard. This produces a so-called molding resin. Objects such as cups are shaped when this resin is simultaneously heated and compressed in a mold.

Plastics can also be shaped by extrusion and laminating. Pipes, for example, are made by extrusion. A screwlike device forces molten plastic through the hole in a die. Plastic sheet is made by extruding molten plastic through a ring-shaped slit. Heatproof surfaces are made by laminating: sandwiching together layers of material soaked in thermosetting plastic resin.

Vacuum forming

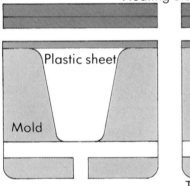
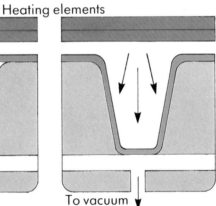

A sheet of plastic is placed on top of the mold and heated until it is soft. The mold is then connected to a vacuum line, and the air is sucked out of it. Outside air pressure forces the plastic into the mold.

Blow molding

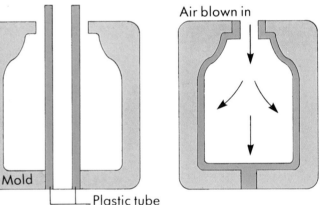

A length of hot plastic tubing is placed in the open mold. This then closes and seals the bottom. Air is blown into the tube from above, forcing the plastic against the walls of the mold.

Injection molding

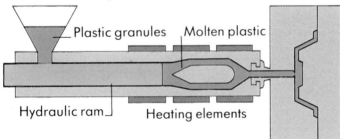

Plastic granules are fed into the injection-molding machine and heated until they melt. A hydraulic ram then forces the molten plastic into the water-cooled mold, where it cools and sets.

Extrusion

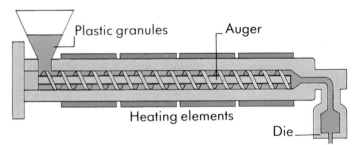

In the extrusion machine, plastic granules are heated until they melt. A screwlike device called an auger rotates and forces the molten plastic through a shaped hole called a die.

Artificial fibers

Silk, the finest natural fiber, is produced, or "spun," by the silkworm. In 1884 a French chemist, Hilaire Chardonnet, succeeded in imitating the silkworm and produced long fibers of what he called artificial silk. The material he used was cellulose nitrate. To make the fibers, he dissolved it in a solvent. He then forced the solution through the fine holes of a device similar to the spinning gland of the silkworm. Fibers formed when the solvent evaporated from the fine streams of solution.

In 1892 a better method of making artificial silk was developed: the viscose process. It produced fibers of pure cellulose. This process is still very important today, producing fibers called viscose, or viscose rayon. The cellulose is treated first with caustic soda and then with carbon disulfide. Fibers form when the cellulose solution is pumped through a spinneret into an acid bath. There the cellulose is regenerated. Acetate and triacetate are similar fibers made from cellulose acetates.

Many fibers used today, however, are wholly synthetic. They are kinds of plastics that can be drawn out into continuous threads, or filaments. Synthetic fibers are very strong, do not rot or absorb water, and are not attacked by insects. Among the best-known are nylon, polyester, and acrylic fibers. Nylon and polyester fibers are produced by melt spinning – forcing molten plastic through a spinneret. The acrylics are produced from a solution of plastic.

Making nylon fiber

In this method, nylon polymer is made from caprolactam. Then nylon chips are melted and spun into fibers, which are stretched and crimped.

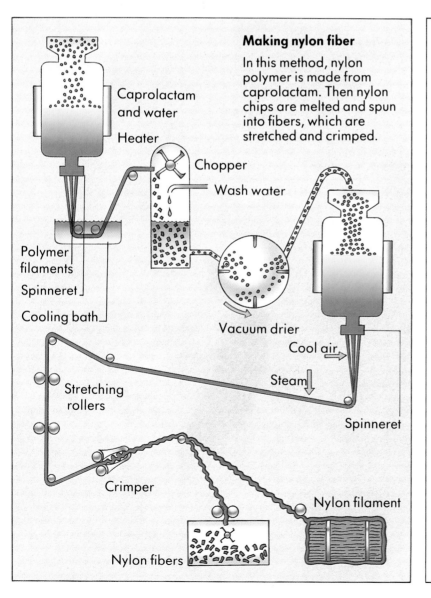

Caprolactam and water

Heater

Chopper

Wash water

Polymer filaments

Spinneret

Cooling bath

Vacuum drier

Cool air

Steam

Stretching rollers

Spinneret

Crimper

Nylon filament

Nylon fibers

The nylon man

In the early 1930s an American chemist, Wallace H. Carothers, headed a research team trying to find a substitute for silk. Carothers eventually found two coal-tar chemicals, adipic acid and hexamethylenediamine, that would copolymerize to form molecules like those of silk. He produced the first practical fiber from the polymer in 1935. It was the first synthetic fiber which was fine and lustrous, elastic and strong. It came to be called nylon.

Food and drugs

Spot facts

• A strain of "super rat" is now breeding which can resist pesticides such as warfarin.

• The synthetic sweetener saccharin (the cyclic imide of ortho-sulfobenzoic acid) is 550 times sweeter than ordinary sugar.

• Aspirin (acetylsalicylic acid) is the world's commonest drug. People in the United States alone take 4 metric tons of aspirin tablets every day to treat colds and headaches.

• Digitalis, a heart stimulant, is one of the oldest drugs still in use. It is prepared from the dried leaves of the purple foxglove.

Chemical processing plays a major part in the daily lives of most people in developed countries. Farmers apply chemical fertilizers to the soil to make their crops grow better and produce greater yields. They spray the crops with chemicals to kill insects and protect against disease. Our food is often treated with chemicals so that it looks and tastes more appetizing, and can be kept for longer periods without deteriorating. Methods of food preservation enable us to enjoy a wider range of foods. Without the benefit of synthetic drugs, we would succumb to all manner of diseases.

► A doctor injects a drug into a patient with a hypodermic syringe. The body of the syringe carries a graduated scale, allowing an accurate dose of the drug to be administered. A subcutaneous injection goes under the skin. An intravenous injection, such as this, goes into a vein.

Agricultural chemicals

When crops grow, they extract nutrients from the soil. To ensure that the soil remains fertile, these nutrients must be replaced. This is done by applying fertilizers. In the early days of farming, animal manure was enough. Nowadays chemical fertilizers, such as superphosphate and ammonium compounds, are used.

Growing crops can be attacked by many insect pests and also many fungal diseases. Again, the chemist comes to the aid of the farmer by creating powerful insecticides and fungicides. Competition with weeds is also eliminated by means of herbicides (weed killers). Many of the most potent pesticides are chlorinated hydrocarbons, such as dieldrin and DDT. These chemicals are deadly to animal life, and once in the food chain, their effects accumulate. Other effective pesticides, including organic phosphorus compounds, are less toxic to animal life and are not so persistent.

◄ Chemical herbicide has been sprayed around this young oil palm to kill weed growth. This gives the palm room to establish itself.

▼ An Asian farmer sprays insecticide on a grain crop to prevent insect pests from breeding and multiplying.

Food technology

Most of the foods we eat have been processed in some way. Even fresh foods such as fruits may have been treated with chemicals to assist ripening. Food processing began thousands of years ago, when early peoples began to make bread from the grain crops they gathered. Bread is still one of the basic foodstuffs of the world, and has been called the "staff of life."

The principles of making bread have hardly changed over the years, although it is now often mass-produced in factories. Bread is made by baking a prepared dough in a hot oven. The dough is a mixture of flour, salt, and water, to which yeast has been added to make it ferment. The fermenting yeast produces carbon dioxide gas, which makes the dough rise. This gives

▼ Fermentation tanks at a distillery. In these tanks sugars extracted from grain are fermented with yeast. The yeast changes the sugars into alcohol, with carbon dioxide bubbling off as a waste product.

bread its typical light texture when it is baked.

From early times fermentation has also been used for another purpose, making beer. Beer is produced by fermenting watery mixtures of grains. The yeast turns sugar extracted from the grain into alcohol, while carbon dioxide is given off as a waste product. This reaction was probably the first chemical process utilized by man.

Like bread, milk has been part of our staple diet since the beginning of civilization. And it has also been processed into other foodstuffs for nearly as long. One is butter. This is made by churning the cream that settles on top of the milk. Churning – rotating the cream in a drum – causes the little fat globules in the cream to join together into a solid mass, butter. Cheese is another food derived from milk. It is made by adding rennet to milk, which makes it set into a solid curd. This then matures into cheese.

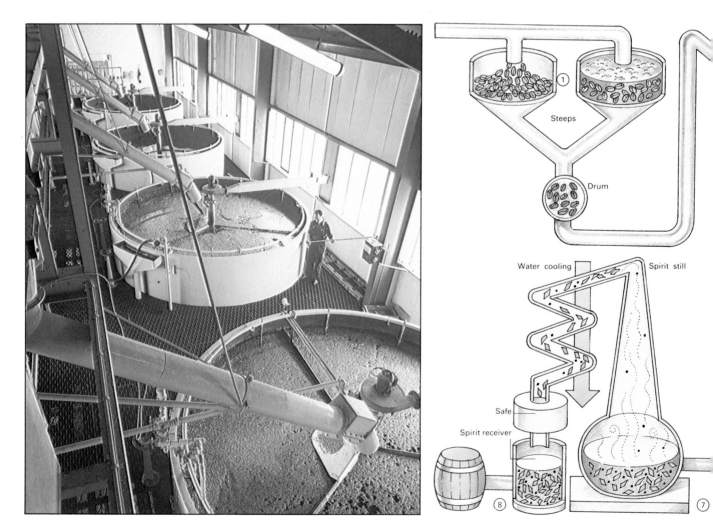

We can think of cheese making as a way of preserving milk, which otherwise turns sour in a day or so. It would get sour even sooner were it not for a treatment it receives in the dairy before bottling or packaging. This treatment is pasteurization, which involves the milk being heated briefly, then quickly cooled.

Several other methods are used to preserve food. They all aim to halt or slow down the processes that cause food to spoil. Spoilage may be brought about by microorganisms, such as bacteria, or by chemical changes. Traditional methods of preservation include smoking, pickling, and drying. The commonest methods of preservation are canning and freezing.

▶ Filling cans with fish in a canning factory. The cans will next be sealed, and then sterilized by heating in batches.

Making malt whisky

The making of Scotch whisky is a lengthy process. The first step is malting, which involves soaking barley until it germinates, or starts to grow shoots (1). The malted barley is then dried in a kiln (2). After being weighed, the dried barley is ground up (3) and mixed with hot water to form mash (4). The sugar (maltose) in the grain passes into solution to form a liquid called wort. After filtering and cooling, the wort is fermented with yeast (5) for about two days. The liquid is then distilled (6), producing a weak alcohol and water solution. This solution is distilled again (7), producing a "spirit" with a high alcoholic content (8).

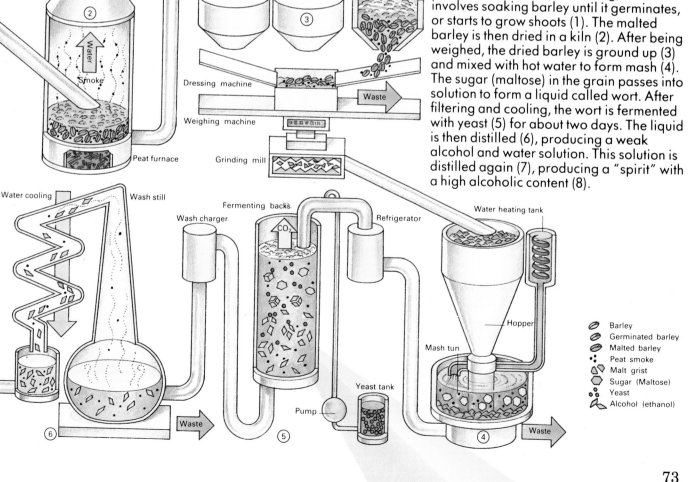

Synthetic foods

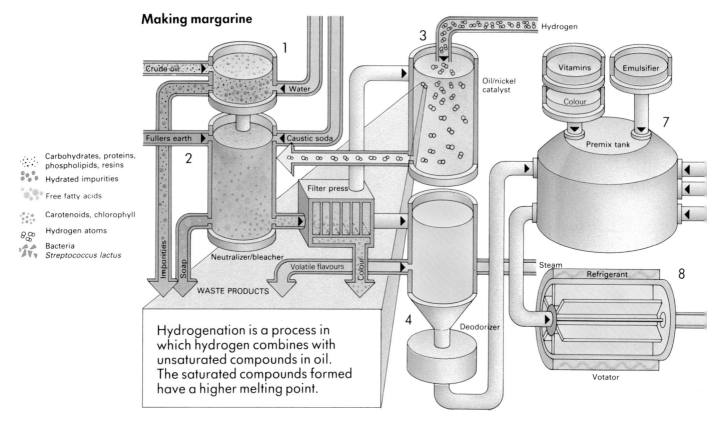

Making margarine

Carbohydrates, proteins, phospholipids, resins

Hydrated impurities

Free fatty acids

Carotenoids, chlorophyll

Hydrogen atoms

Bacteria *Streptococcus lactus*

Crude oil

Water

Fullers earth

Caustic soda

Hydrogen

Oil/nickel catalyst

Vitamins

Emulsifier

Colour

Premix tank

Filter press

Impurities

Soap

Neutralizer/bleacher

Volatile flavours

Colour

WASTE PRODUCTS

Deodorizer

Steam

Refrigerant

Votator

Hydrogenation is a process in which hydrogen combines with unsaturated compounds in oil. The saturated compounds formed have a higher melting point.

In 1869 a French chemist named Hippolyte Mège-Mouriès patented one of the first synthetic foods. He called it margarine, a name possibly based on his surname. It won him a contest launched by Emperor Napoleon III to find a palatable substitute for butter. Mège-Mouriès made his margarine using fats from beef suet, pig's stomach, and cow's udder. He mixed with them skim milk or whey.

Animal fats are still used to make some margarines. But most are made using vegetable oils, including safflower, sunflower, coconut, and palm oils. These oils are converted during manufacture into solid fats by treatment with hydrogen. Margarines based on vegetable oils now sell very well because it is widely believed that they are healthier to eat than butter and other animal fat products.

Margarine contains various additives which give it the right consistency, improve its nutritional value, help preserve it, and enhance its appearance. They include emulsifiers, which prevent the fats and water in the margarine from separating out. An important emulsifier is lecithin, found in egg yolks. Vitamins A and D may be added to increase food value.

The color in margarines comes from a dye called beta carotene, which occurs naturally in carrots. But most of this coloring is now made synthetically from coal tar. Potassium sorbate is a common preservative found in margarines.

Emulsifiers, vitamins, coloring, and preservatives are common additives found in most processed foods today. Other additives include thickeners, such as gelatin and alginates (extracted from seaweed), and antioxidants. These are mainly synthetic compounds that stop fats from going rancid and keep other foods from developing unpleasant flavors. Monosodium glutamate is a common additive that brings out the flavor of food. Sweetness is provided by the addition of glucose or other sugars, or by synthetic sweeteners such as aspartame and saccharin.

Synthetic proteins include meat substitutes, actually a form of textured vegetable protein (TVP). The vegetable involved here is the soybean. Protein is extracted from the beans and then dissolved in alkali. The solution is then extruded through a spinneret into an acid bath. The protein emerges as fibers, which are gathered into a rope and then chopped.

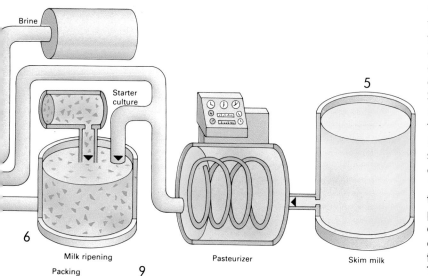

◀ Margarine is now made mainly from vegetable oil. The impure, or crude, oil is washed with water (1) and then treated with caustic soda and fuller's earth (2). The alkali combines with unwanted substances to form a soap. The fuller's earth removes color. Some oils require treatment with hydrogen to make them solid (3). Steam is then bubbled through the purified oil in a deodorizer (4) to remove any remaining odor. Meanwhile, skim milk is being prepared in another part of the plant (5). After being pasteurized, it is "ripened" by treatment with bacteria (6). It then passes with the oil and brine into the premix tank (7). Other ingredients are also added at this stage. These may include colorings, to give a "buttery" color; vitamins, to improve food value; and an emulsifier. The margarine mixture solidifies in a refrigerated rotating device called a votator (8) and passes to the packing machine (9).

Brine

Starter culture

5

6

Milk ripening

Packing

9

Pasteurizer

Skim milk

The food chemist

Chemists help food manufacturers ensure that their products look good, taste good, have a long shelf life, and, above all, are safe. Food chemists (inset) study, for example, how the body recognizes flavors and the mechanisms of food decay. They develop additives to improve flavor, arrest decay, and so on.

They also analyze natural flavorings, which they try to imitate or improve upon by chemical synthesis. In their analysis they often use a technique called chromatography to separate out the chemicals in a substance. An analysis of natural peppermint oil (left) shows that menthol, menthone, and methyl acetate are the main ingredients. A mixture of these chemicals would produce an artificial peppermint flavor very similar to that of the natural product.

In many countries all additives in food products must be listed on the label. In Europe they are usually identified by an E number, which indicates that they have been approved for use in EEC (European Economic Community) countries.

Menthol

Solvent

Methyl acetate

Menthone

Isomenthone
Menthofuran

Octan-3-ol

Making drugs

Penicillin

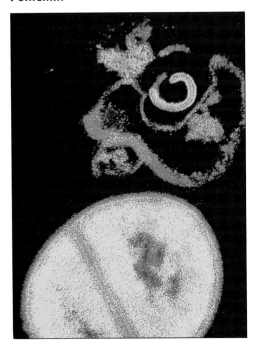

The original antibiotic, penicillin, is produced by the *Penicillium* mold. It is still widely used to combat diseases caused by such bacteria as staphylococcus, which causes boils and abcesses. The picture shows at bottom a normal staphylococcus bacterium, and at top a bacterium that has been destroyed by penicillin. Penicillin works by breaking up the bacterium's outer membrane.

◀ Traditionally, drugs were prepared using minerals and plant extracts. Some, such as tincture of iodine and digitalis (from foxgloves), are still used. But most medicines are now manufactured.

▲ Opium poppies growing in Thailand. Opium is harvested by cutting the pods and collecting the liquid that oozes out (inset). The pain-killing properties of opium have been known for over 2,000 years.

▶ A technician tends a fermentation vessel in a biotechnology plant, which produces disease-fighting antibodies from cultured cells. These antibodies are used to help diagnose diseases.

Today doctors have at their disposal a vast array of medicines, or drugs, with which they can successfully treat most of the diseases that affect us. Drugs are also known as pharmaceuticals. They may be derived from plants, animals, and minerals, or made from chemicals.

Opium, obtained from poppy seeds, is probably the oldest known effective drug. Opium and drugs made from it – codeine, morphine, and heroin – are powerful analgesics, or pain-relievers. But they are highly addictive. This means that people who take them regularly develop a craving for them, and find it very hard to stop taking them.

Quinine is a well-known plant drug used to treat malaria. It was obtained originally from the bark of the cinchona tree of South America. But most is now manufactured synthetically.

The manufacture of synthetic drugs dates from the late 1890s, when the Bayer chemical company in Germany began manufacturing aspirin on a large scale from coal-tar chemicals. Among other powerful synthetic drugs, the sulfonamides, or sulfa drugs, are outstanding. They fight many bacterial infections.

Among drugs obtained from animals, the hormone insulin is best known. It is extracted from the pancreas of cattle and pigs, and is used to treat diabetes.

Antibiotics are perhaps the most powerful weapons against disease. Alexander Fleming discovered the original antibiotic, penicillin, in 1928. It went into widespread production in the early 1940s. The antibiotics can now treat diseases such as pneumonia and typhoid, which in the past were generally fatal.

Everyday industries

Spot facts

● Books printed in the 1400s on parchment made from animal skin are in better condition than books printed early this century on wood pulp paper, which tends to rot.

● The latest rotor-spinning machines can produce 150 m (500 ft.) of spun yarn per minute.

● The English chemist William H. Perkin made the first synthetic dye in 1856, while trying to synthesize the antimalaria drug quinine.

● Today's silicon chips may contain up to half a million or more transistors and other electronic components. Yet they are only about the same size as a single transistor of the 1950s.

The invention of paper in China about 105 AD can be considered a key invention in the development of civilization. It provided, in the course of time, our first means of mass communication and mass education through books, newspapers, and magazines.

Spinning and weaving are two of the most ancient crafts, dating back at least 10,000 years. Until about 200 years ago, they were practiced at home on simple machines, such as the spinning wheel and hand loom. In many countries, they still are. Then in the 1700s more productive spinning and weaving machines were invented. These took textile making out of the home, and it became the first factory industry.

▶ Machines in a modern factory work automatically under the control of a computer, or "electronic brain". Individual machines may even have their own "brains", in the guise of a silicon chip.

Pulp and paper

Until about 150 years ago, most paper was made from linen and rags, materials that are still used to make the best-quality writing paper. But increasing demand for paper, for books and newspapers, led to wood in the form of wood pulp becoming the main raw material.

Wood pulp is made mainly from softwoods such as pine and spruces. It can be made in two ways. Groundwood pulp is made by shredding logs in a huge grinding machine. This results in a coarse pulp suitable only for making newsprint, the paper on which newspapers are printed. Chemical pulp is used to produce better-quality paper. It is made by "digesting" wood chips in a solution of chemicals, usually sodium sulfate. The chemical treatment frees the wood fibers from their binder (lignin).

Wood pulp is usually transported to the paper mill as dry bales. And so the first stage in papermaking is to mix the pulp with water to convert it back into a liquid state. The liquid pulp then feeds into a machine in which sets of revolving knives beat and fray the wood fibers. This enables them to bind together better later.

Next, the beaten pulp goes into a mixer tank, where it is blended with materials that will determine the quality and appearance of the finished paper. They include a filler, such as china clay, to give the paper "body" and make it smoother; "size," or resin glue, to make the paper easier to write and print on; and maybe dyes or pigments to add color.

The prepared watery pulp then passes to the papermaking machine, the Fourdrinier machine. It flows onto a wire-mesh belt, where the water drains or is sucked away. The damp web that forms is then squeezed by heavy rollers before being fed around steam-heated cylinders to dry. After a final rolling by heavy calender rolls, the paper is wound onto reels.

Papermaking

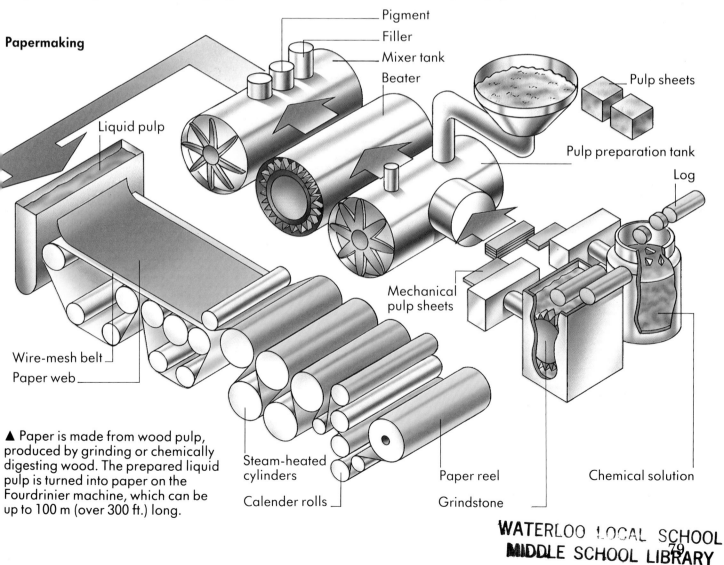

Pigment
Filler
Mixer tank
Beater
Pulp sheets
Pulp preparation tank
Log
Liquid pulp
Mechanical pulp sheets
Wire-mesh belt
Paper web
Chemical solution
Steam-heated cylinders
Paper reel
Calender rolls
Grindstone

▲ Paper is made from wood pulp, produced by grinding or chemically digesting wood. The prepared liquid pulp is turned into paper on the Fourdrinier machine, which can be up to 100 m (over 300 ft.) long.

Textiles

Textiles are materials made from fibers. The most common material is cloth, made by weaving long threads, called yarns. Yarn is made by drawing out and twisting "ropes" of fibers, a process called spinning.

The traditional fibers for making cloth come from animals and plants. More and more these days, however, synthetic fibers are used instead. They are made by processing natural materials, such as cellulose, or are manufactured wholly from chemicals.

The original fiber used was wool, which comes from the fleece of sheep. It is a kind of hair that is naturally curly. The Merino breed produces the finest wool and the heaviest fleece. The fleeces of some goats, such as the Angora and Cashmere breeds, also yields excellent fibers.

Another prized animal fiber, silk, has quite a different origin. It is produced by the silkworm, the larva stage of a moth. Unlike other natural fibers, which are short, silk is produced as a continuous thread, or filament.

Cotton is by far the most important plant fiber, obtained from the boll, or fluffy seed head of the cotton plant. Flax is a grasslike plant that has fibers in its stem. They are made into the fabric we call linen. Other natural fibers include jute and asbestos.

Spinning

With the exception of silk, the fibers from plants and animals are relatively short, usually just a few centimeters long. To make them suitable for making textiles, they must be spun into continuous yarn. Before the actual spinning process can begin, the fibers must be carefully prepared.

In the case of cotton, the bales are first opened and the fluffy bolls are broken down into a loose fiber blanket called lap. This is then fed into a carding machine, which removes the very short fibers and also straightens out the long ones. For the best-quality yarn the fibers are straightened further by combing. They emerge from the combing machine as a web, which is then gathered into a loose rope, called sliver. Several slivers are combined and drawn out through rotating rollers to form roving. The roving goes to the spinning frame, where it is drawn out and given a twist for strength.

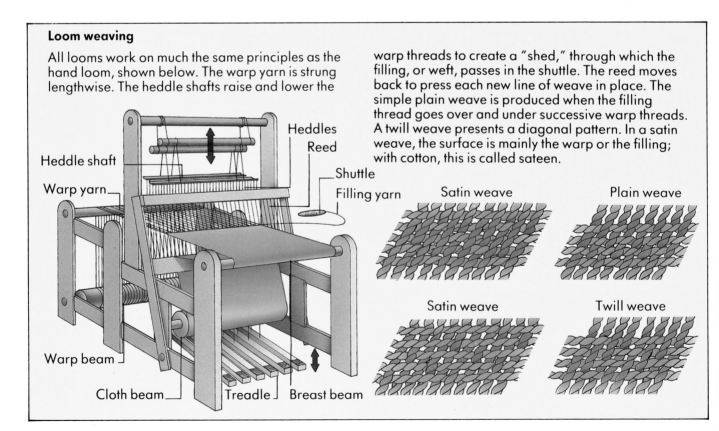

Loom weaving

All looms work on much the same principles as the hand loom, shown below. The warp yarn is strung lengthwise. The heddle shafts raise and lower the warp threads to create a "shed," through which the filling, or weft, passes in the shuttle. The reed moves back to press each new line of weave in place. The simple plain weave is produced when the filling thread goes over and under successive warp threads. A twill weave presents a diagonal pattern. In a satin weave, the surface is mainly the warp or the filling; with cotton, this is called sateen.

Heddles
Reed
Heddle shaft
Warp yarn
Shuttle
Filling yarn
Warp beam
Cloth beam
Treadle
Breast beam

Satin weave
Plain weave
Satin weave
Twill weave

Weaving

Weaving takes place on a loom, on which one set of threads (the warp) is stretched lengthwise on a frame. The weaving process consists of passing thread (the filling, or weft) crosswise through a gap (the shed), created by raising and lowering sets of warp threads. Different patterns of weave are produced according to how the warp threads are separated. On traditional looms the filling is carried through the warp in a shuttle. But in the latest looms, rapierlike rods and even jets of air or water are used to carry the filling. On some looms, over 400 m (1,300 ft.) of filling can be put down each minute.

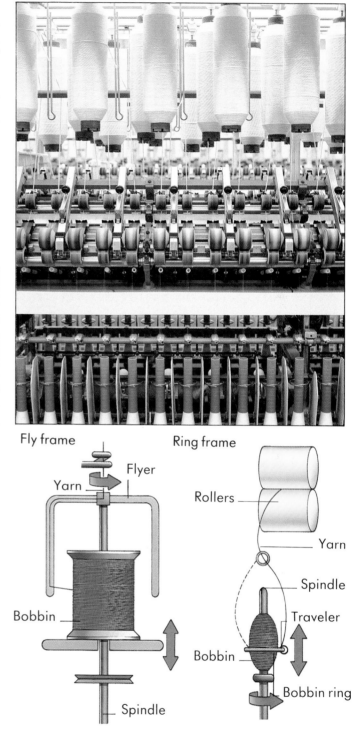

Dazzling dyes

Textiles have been made more attractive by dyeing for at least 5,000 years. Until the mid-1800s textile manufacturers had to rely on natural dyes, extracted mainly from plants.

In 1856, however, the English chemist William H. Perkin accidentally produced a new dye while experimenting with aniline, a liquid extracted then from coal tar. He called the new dye mauveine, which had the color we now call mauve (see picture). It was the first synthetic dye.

▲ (top) The final stage of spinning worsted yarn. Worsted is produced using only long wool fibers. Two common spinning machines are the fly and ring frames (bottom). On the fly frame, the yarn is twisted as the flyer spins around at high speed, dragging the bobbin with it. On the ring frame drawn-out yarn is wound onto the bobbin and given a twist as the traveler moves around the ring.

Transportation

The revolution in industry began in textile manufacturing, and gathered pace at the end of the 1700s. Throughout the 1800s, transportation also underwent a revolution. First came the railroads, on which new locomotives could haul enormous loads. These locomotives had engines powered by steam. Steam engines also took to the water, making shipping faster and more reliable.

By the end of the 1800s, road transportation began to improve, with the development of the automobile. Air transportation, in the form of balloons and airships, had also begun. But the real breakthrough in air transportation came when the Wright brothers in the United States built the first power-driven airplane in 1903.

Transportation by water tends to be very slow, because of friction with the water. In general, ships today are not much faster than they were a century ago. Hovercraft and hydrofoils are new kinds of vessels which have been successful in increasing the speed of travel over water. They are only used on short trips.

In traditional shipbuilding, hulls are usually constructed from steel plates welded together. The hull is not built up plate by plate. Large sections are built first and then put together afterward. Fiberglass-reinforced plastic and even concrete hulls are also made.

Railroad construction has not changed much since the pioneering days of the last century. The idea of running a steel-wheeled vehicle on a steel track is a good one because of the low friction between them. Modern rails are made by rolling steel slabs with grooved rollers. The biggest change in railroad practice since the last century is in the power source for the locomotives. Most are now powered by diesel engines or electricity.

The automobile has changed almost beyond

The international Airbus A320

The successful Airbus A320 is manufactured piecemeal in plants spread throughout Europe. In Great Britain, British Aerospace makes the wings (left); in France, SNECMA assembles American-designed engines and Aérospatiale makes the nose and cockpit; in Germany MBB makes the fuselage and tail fin; in the Netherlands, Fokker makes the movable surfaces on the wings; and in Spain, CASA makes the tail plane.

All the prefabricated units are transported to Aérospatiale's plant at Toulouse in southwest France, where they are assembled on a production line (right). The larger parts are delivered by the bulbous Super Guppy.

recognition. The success of the automobile has been a triumph for manufacturing industry. The early automobiles were built by hand in small numbers. Today's cars are produced in the millions. The automotive industry was the first to introduce assembly lines, automation, and robots.

Whereas most ships, locomotives, and cars are constructed mainly of steel, most aircraft are built of aluminum alloys. These alloys are as strong as steel, but very much lighter. The aluminum sheets and other structures in the airframe, or aircraft body, are put together mainly by riveting. The method of construction, termed "fail-safe," uses staggered joints and other devices to prevent dangerous cracks from running through the structure. Synthetic adhesives are also being used in airframe construction. Even the fuselage of some aircraft is now made of synthetic composites.

▶ Robot machines weld together steel sections to form the body shells on a car production line. Robot welders work with greater precision than humans, and are not affected by the heat and glare.

▼ The main hull and deck structure of a ship nearing completion at Ancona in Italy. Like all big ships, it is constructed of welded steel plates. When the hull is finished and painted, the ship will be ready to launch.

Electronics

Electronics is concerned with devices that control the flow of electrons in substances. It puts electrons to work in various ways. For example, it makes them create pictures on a TV screen, do mathematical operations in a calculator, work a computer, guide a robot, and play a compact disk.

Electronics today deals with the flow of electricity not so much through wires, but through substances that hardly conduct electricity at all. We call them semiconductors. The most important semiconductor by far is silicon. This element does not conduct electricity at all when it is pure, but it does – a little – when tiny amounts of impurities are added to it.

By adding different impurities to it, silicon can be given two electrical states, called n-type and p-type. By linking bits of the two types together, electronic devices like transistors,

capacitors, and resistors can be made. And they can be linked, or integrated, into circuits that can work TVs, calculators, or computers.

There has been a revolution in electronics during the last few decades because these integrated circuits can now be made microscopically small. A wafer of silicon the size of a shirt button can carry hundreds of thousands of components and by itself run computers and other electronic equipment. We call these wafers silicon chips or microchips. A typical chip is only about 6 mm (¼ in.) square and about one-tenth of a millimeter thick, and it weighs less than one-hundredth of a gram (⅓,₀₀₀ oz.).

Making chips
A chip is designed so that its components and circuits can be built up in layers. There are layers of n-type and p-type silicon; a number of

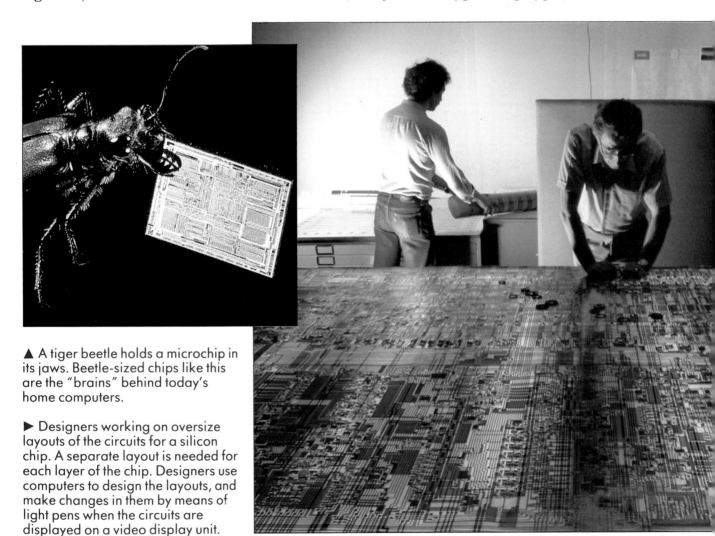

▲ A tiger beetle holds a microchip in its jaws. Beetle-sized chips like this are the "brains" behind today's home computers.

▶ Designers working on oversize layouts of the circuits for a silicon chip. A separate layout is needed for each layer of the chip. Designers use computers to design the layouts, and make changes in them by means of light pens when the circuits are displayed on a video display unit.

conducting and insulating layers; and a final metallic layer (usually aluminum) to provide connections. The components and pathways between them are required only in certain parts of each layer. So the other areas have to be masked off. Masks are made for each layer by photographically reducing the circuit layout used by designers to 1/250 of its size.

The starting point for making chips is a slice of ultrapure silicon crystal about 15 cm (6 in.) across. This has space for several hundred chips. The first stage of processing is to treat, or "dope," the slice with chemical vapor (often boron) to create p-type silicon. The slice is then heated in a steam oven to give it an insulating layer of silicon dioxide.

A series of photographic masking and etching processes then follows; one for each layer. They create "windows" through which the silicon can

be treated. In the first masking stage, for example, areas of silicon dioxide are stripped away to allow doping of the silicon by phosphorus vapor, which creates n-type regions.

In all, more than two dozen stages of masking, doping, etching, and so on, are required in making chips. Afterward, each chip on the slice is carefully tested and inspected. As many as one in four may be rejected as a result.

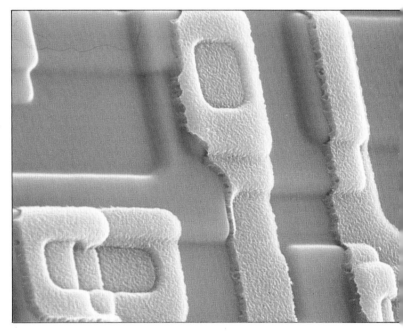

▶ A small section of the circuitry on a silicon chip, magnified about 4,000 times.

▼ Slices of silicon containing finished chips being inspected under the microscope. Next, they will be cut up, and the good chips will go for mounting. Many will be rejected.

▲ Computers and other electronic equipment are assembled from circuit boards like this. The various electronic components are mounted on an insulated board and connected by printed circuits, made up of films of copper. This method of assembly simplifies troubleshooting.

Units of measurement

Units of measurement

This encyclopedia gives measurements in metric units, which are commonly used in science. Approximate equivalents in traditional American units, sometimes called U.S. customary units, are also given in the text, in parentheses.

Some common metric and U.S. units

Here are some equivalents, accurate to parts per million. For many practical purposes rougher equivalents may be adequate, especially when the quantity being converted from one system to the other is known with an accuracy of just one or two digits. Equivalents marked with an asterisk (*) are exact.

Volume
1 cubic centimeter = 0.0610237 cubic inch
1 cubic meter = 35.3147 cubic feet
1 cubic meter = 1.30795 cubic yards
1 cubic kilometer = 0.239913 cubic mile

1 cubic inch = 16.3871 cubic centimeters
1 cubic foot = 0.0283168 cubic meter
1 cubic yard = 0.764555 cubic meter

Liquid measure
1 milliliter = 0.0338140 fluidounce
1 liter = 1.05669 quarts

1 fluidounce = 29.5735 milliliters
1 quart = 0.946353 liter

Mass and weight
1 gram = 0.0352740 ounce
1 kilogram = 2.20462 pounds
1 metric ton = 1.10231 short tons

1 ounce = 28.3495 grams
1 pound = 0.453592 kilogram
1 short ton = 0.907185 metric ton

Length
1 millimeter = 0.0393701 inch
1 centimeter = 0.393701 inch
1 meter = 3.28084 feet
1 meter = 1.09361 yards
1 kilometer = 0.621371 mile

1 inch = 2.54* centimeters
1 foot = 0.3048* meter
1 yard = 0.9144* meter
1 mile = 1.60934 kilometers

Area
1 square centimeter = 0.155000 square inch
1 square meter = 10.7639 square feet
1 square meter = 1.19599 square yards
1 square kilometer = 0.386102 square mile

1 square inch = 6.4516* square centimeters
1 square foot = 0.0929030 square meter
1 square yard = 0.836127 square meter
1 square mile = 2.58999 square kilometers

1 hectare = 2.47105 acres
1 acre = 0.404686 hectare

Temperature conversions

To convert temperatures in degrees Celsius to temperatures in degrees Fahrenheit, or vice versa, use these formulas:

Celsius Temperature = (Fahrenheit Temperature − 32) × 5/9
Fahrenheit Temperature = (Celsius Temperature × 9/5) + 32

Numbers and abbreviations

Numbers

Scientific measurements sometimes involve extremely large numbers. Scientists often express large numbers in a concise "exponential" form using powers of 10. The number one billion, or 1,000,000,000, if written in this form, would be 10^9; three billion, or 3,000,000,000, would be 3×10^9. The "exponent" 9 tells you that there are nine zeros following the 3. More complicated numbers can be written in this way by using decimals; for example, 3.756×10^9 is the same as 3,756,000,000.

Very small numbers – numbers close to zero – can be written in exponential form with a minus sign on the exponent. For example, one-billionth, which is 1/1,000,000,000 or 0.000000001, would be 10^{-9}. Here, the 9 in the exponent -9 tells you that, in the decimal form of the number, the 1 is in the ninth place to the right of the decimal point. Three-billionths, or 3/1,000,000,000, would be 3×10^{-9}; accordingly, 3.756×10^{-9} would mean 0.000000003756 (or 3.756/1,000,000,000).

Here are the American names of some powers of ten, and how they are written in numerals:

1 million (10^6)	1,000,000
1 billion (10^9)	1,000,000,000
1 trillion (10^{12})	1,000,000,000,000
1 quadrillion (10^{15})	1,000,000,000,000,000
1 quintillion (10^{18})	1,000,000,000,000,000,000
1 sextillion (10^{21})	1,000,000,000,000,000,000,000
1 septillion (10^{24})	1,000,000,000,000,000,000,000,000

Principal abbreviations used in the encyclopedia

°C	degrees Celsius		kg	kilogram
cc	cubic centimeter		l	liter
cm	centimeter		lb.	pound
cu.	cubic		m	meter
d	days		mi.	mile
°F	degrees Fahrenheit		ml	milliliter
fl. oz.	fluidounce		mm	millimeter
fps	feet per second		mph	miles per hour
ft.	foot		mps	miles per second
g	gram		mya	millions of years ago
h	hour		N	north
Hz	hertz		oz.	ounce
in.	inch		qt.	quart
K	kelvin (degree temperature)		s	second
			S	south
			sq.	square
			V	volt
			y	year
			yd.	yard

Glossary

acetate A textile fiber related to rayon and in which the fibers are of cellulose acetate or triacetate.

alloy A mixture of metals, or of a metal and a nonmetal. Brass is a common alloy, made from copper and zinc.

anode A positive electrode; for example, of an electric cell.

antibiotic A compound that is produced by a microorganism, such as a mold, and that can kill bacteria that cause disease.

aromatics Organic compounds related to benzene that contain a benzene-ring structure.

artificial fibers Fibers produced by processing natural materials and also those produced wholly from chemicals.

asbestos Any of certain minerals that occur naturally in the form of fibers.

assembly line A method of production in which workers add parts to a product as it moves past them on a conveyor.

automation The widespread introduction of automatic machines into industry.

Bakelite The first completely synthetic plastic, named after its inventor, Leo H. Baekeland.

biogenic deposits Mineral deposits formed from the remains of once-living organisms.

biotechnology Methods of producing biological materials such as antibiotics on an industrial scale.

blast furnace The furnace in which iron and other metals are smelted. It is named for the blast of hot air that makes the furnace burn fiercely.

blow molding A method of shaping hollow plastic objects by blowing air into the middle of molten plastic within a mold.

bottled gas Properly called liquefied petroleum gas, or LPG; gas extracted from natural gas that can be readily liquefied under pressure. It is usually propane or butane.

brazing A method of joining metal parts by melting between them a noniron "filler" metal that has a lower melting point than the two metals being joined. If the filler's melting point is below 427°C (800°F), the process is called soldering.

bronze A most useful alloy, being a mixture of copper and tin. It was the first metal widely used, beginning about 3500 BC, and it ushered in a period of history known as the Bronze Age.

casting A method of shaping metal by pouring it as a red-hot liquid into a mold and allowing it to cool.

catalyst A substance that increases (or decreases) the rate of a chemical reaction without changing chemically itself.

cathode A negative electrode; for example, in an electric cell. In general it is a source of electrons.

celluloid The first plastic, made from cellulose nitrate, with a little added camphor.

ceramics Materials made by heating nonmetallic substances in a furnace or kiln. Pottery, cement, and glass are familiar ceramic products.

cermet A combination of a ceramic and a metal; used for its heat resistance in jet and rocket engines.

coal tar A tarry substance obtained by destructively distilling coal – that is, by heating it at high temperatures in the absence of air. Coal tar was once the main source of organic chemicals.

composite A synthetic material, consisting usually of a plastic reinforced with a fiber, such as glass or carbon fibers.

compression molding A method of shaping thermosetting plastics by the simultaneous application of heat and pressure.

copolymer A polymer made from different monomers. The commonest synthetic rubber is made of a copolymer of butadiene and styrene.

cracking An oil-refinery process in which heavy oil fractions are broken down into lighter, more useful ones. It may be brought about with the help of a catalyst or steam. Steam cracking produces a wide variety of chemical raw materials.

DDT The compound dichlorodiphenyltrichloroethane, a powerful insecticide. Its use is now restricted because it is toxic to higher forms of life and is very persistent – it remains in the environment for a long time.

die A metal mold.

die-casting Casting molten metal into a shape by forcing the metal into a metal mold, or die.

distillation A process in which a liquid is heated until it turns into vapor, which is then condensed back into liquid by cooling. It is a common method of separating and purifying liquids.

doping Treating a silicon chip with a chemical vapor to make it conduct electricity.

drug A natural or synthetic product that affects the working of the body in some way.

ductility A property of a metal that enables it to be drawn out into fine wire without breaking.

duralumin An aluminum alloy containing copper, magnesium, and manganese. It shows the property of age-hardening, gradually hardening for several days after it has been made.

electrolysis Splitting up a compound in solution or when molten by passing an electric current through it. It is a useful way of producing or refining some metals, including aluminum and copper.

electrometallurgy Using electrolysis to extract or refine metals.

electronics The branch of science concerned with devices that control the flow of electrons, as in computers, TV, and radio.

elements, chemical Simple substances made up of atoms with the same atomic number. They are the building blocks of matter.

evaporites Mineral deposits laid down when salty seas evaporated. Deposits of rock salt and gypsum formed in this way.

extrusion A method of making plastic rods and pipes by forcing molten plastic through a die.

factory A place in which goods are made, usually with the help of machines.

fermentation A process in which yeast acts upon starch or sugar to produce alcohol and carbon dioxide.

fiberglass The common name for a synthetic composite made by reinforcing plastic with glass fibers.

flotation A common method of mineral dressing, used to separate ore particles from impurities. Crushed ore is mixed with a frothing liquid, and the ore particles float to the surface with the bubbles.

forging Shaping metal by hammering or pressing.

fractionation Fractional distillation; a method of distillation which can separate a mixture of liquids (such as crude oil) into various fractions with different boiling points.

FRP Short for fiberglass-reinforced plastic; the proper name for the material we usually call fibreglass.

gangue The earthy and rocky impurities mined with ore.

gem Precious stone; a mineral used in jewelry, which is prized for its color, brilliance, or sparkle. Diamond, sapphire, ruby, emerald, and opal are among the most sought-after gems.

geode A hollow stone or rock that is lined with well-formed crystals.

Haber process One of the most important processes in the chemical industry, the synthesis of ammonia from its component elements – nitrogen and hydrogen. The process is named after the German chemist Fritz Haber, who developed it.

hardwoods Trees, or the timber from trees, which grow in the tropical rain forests (such as ebony and mahogany) and in temperate regions (such as oak and beech).

heavy chemical A chemical produced in vast quantities, such as sulfuric acid and caustic soda.

herbicide A weed killer.

hydraulic press A forging machine which exerts a gradual squeezing action on red-hot metal. It works by means of hydraulic (liquid) pressure.

hydrocarbon A compound made up of hydrogen and carbon only. Petroleum and natural gas are made up almost entirely of hydrocarbons.

hydrometallurgy Extracting metals from their ores by means of chemical solutions.

Industrial Revolution The period of history when the widespread introduction of machines led to the creation of industries.

ingot A metal casting made immediately after smelting, of a convenient size for further shaping

processes.

injection molding A method of shaping plastics by squirting molten plastic into a water-cooled mold.

inorganic chemistry One of the main branches of chemistry, concerned with the study of the chemical elements and their compounds, except carbon compounds containing hydrogen.

integrated circuit A circuit in which all components and pathways are integrated into the same piece of semiconductor, usually silicon.

interchangeable parts Ones that are almost identical. They hold the key to mass production.

Invar An alloy of iron and nickel with traces of other metals. It is unusual in that it expands or contracts hardly at all when the temperature changes.

ion An atom that has lost or gained electrons. In general metals lose electrons to form positive ions, or cations; nonmetals gain electrons to form negative ions, or anions.

lathe The foremost machine tool, on which a machining process called turning is carried out. The workpiece is turned, or rotated, and tools are brought in to remove metal.

leaching Treating a compound with a chemical solution (often an acid) to extract, for example, the metal it contains.

machining Shaping metal by means of machine tools, such as lathes, grinding machines, and milling machines.

magma Molten rock.

malleability A property of a metal that enables it to be hammered into thin sheet without breaking.

margarine A butter substitute made these days mainly from plant oils, such as sunflower oil.

mass production The production of goods on a vast scale, usually by the assembly of interchangeable parts on a production line.

mechanization The introduction of machines, particularly into industry.

metal An element that is typically dense, hard, tough, and shiny; that conducts heat and electricity well; and that can be hammered into a thin sheet or drawn into fine wire without breaking. About three-fourths of the chemical elements are metals, although not all of them have all of the above properties. One, mercury, is a liquid at ordinary temperatures.

metallic mineral One from which a metal can be extracted.

metallurgy The science and technology of metals. Various branches are concerned with the properties of metals, and their extraction, smelting, refining, and shaping.

microchip An alternative name for a silicon chip, particularly a microprocessor, a chip that can act as a computer by itself.

milling A common machining process in which metal is removed by a rotating toothed cutting wheel.

mineral A chemical compound found in the Earth's crust. Every mineral has a definite composition and physical and chemical properties.

mineral dressing Preparation of an ore before smelting. Its main purpose is to concentrate the ore and remove unwanted impurities.

native element An element that is found in a pure state in nature. Gold and carbon are two native elements.

nonmetallic mineral A mineral that may or may not contain a metallic element. If it does contain a metal, its use does not depend on the metal being present.

nugget A lump of native metal, such as a nugget of gold.

open-pit mining Mining on the surface of the ground. See also **strip mining**.

ore A mineral from which metal can profitably be extracted. Many ores are metal oxides or sulfides.

organic chemistry The branch of chemistry concerned with the study of the wealth of carbon compounds containing hydrogen. Such compounds were originally termed "organic" because it was thought that they could be made only by living organisms.

overburden A layer of soil over an ore deposit near the surface of the ground.

panning A method of mining for gold used by early prospectors, in which they swirled a mixture of gravel and water around in a pan.

pasteurization A method of temporarily sterilizing milk and other foods by heating them briefly. It is named after the French chemist who devised it, Louis Pasteur.

petrochemicals Chemicals obtained by processing petroleum in a refinery.

petroleum Crude oil; a greenish-black liquid obtained by drilling into the ground. It is a mixture of thousands of hydrocarbons, which is separated into useful products by refining.

pharmaceuticals Another name for drugs.

pig iron Iron produced in a blast furnace. It contains too many impurities to be useful by itself and so is refined, into steel.

pilot plant A small-scale chemical plant, built to assess the performance of a new process.

placer deposit A deposit of a heavy mineral, such as gold or cassiterite (tin ore), found in stream beds.

plastic A synthetic material made up of long molecules which can be molded into shape by heat.

polymerization A chemical reaction in which a substance with small molecules (a monomer) is converted into a substance with large molecules (a polymer).

printed circuit A circuit made up of a thin layer of copper, which is deposited on a circuit board by a method similar to that used in the production of printing plates.

prospecting Looking for mineral deposits.

prototype A full-sized working model of something, made before full-scale production begins.

quarry A surface mine from which stone, sand, or gravel is extracted.

quartz The most common mineral in the Earth's crust. It is a form of silica, the compound silicon dioxide.

raw materials Basic materials from which other materials are manufactured.

rayon An artificial fiber produced from the cellulose in cotton fibers or wood pulp.

recycling Reprocessing used materials so that they can be used again.

refining Purifying or converting materials into a more useful form – for example, petroleum and metals.

refractories Materials that resist high temperatures.

riveting Joining together pieces of metal by means of headed metal pins.

robot A machine that works automatically under computer control.

salt A chemical compound formed when an acid reacts with a base. Common salt, sodium chloride, is the most familiar salt.

seismic survey A prospecting method in which geologists set up shock waves in the ground, and then record the way they are reflected and refracted (bent) by underground rock layers.

semiconductor A material that conducts electricity slightly when impurities are added to it. Silicon is the most common semiconductor.

silicon chip The name given to a thin wafer of silicon, which carries thousands of electronic circuits, and which can act as part of a computer's circuits, or indeed as a computer itself.

smelting Heating an ore at high temperature in a furnace in order to reduce it to metal.

softwoods Trees, or the timber from trees, which grow mainly in the cold boreal (northerly) regions of the world. They are typically conifers, such as pines, firs, and spruces.

solar evaporation Using the Sun's heat to evaporate water; for example, from seawater in order to extract the salt it contains.

soldering A method of joining metals by melting between them a metal ("solder") that has a melting point below 427°C (800°F). This technique is commonly used for joining copper wires in electronic circuits. Solder most often is a tin-lead alloy.

spinneret The spinning gland of the silkworm; a device for producing artificial fibers, such as rayon.

spinning Drawing out and twisting short fibers to make continuous yarn, or thread.

spoil The waste material excavated from a mine along with the ore.

steel The most important metal by far. It is an iron alloy, containing traces of carbon and other metals, such as manganese.

strip mining A method of surface mining where the material being mined (usually coal) lies below an overburden, which is first removed, or stripped away.

sulfuric acid The most important industrial chemical, with the chemical formula H_2SO_4. It is made by the contact process.

superphosphate A widely used artificial fertilizer made by treating phosphate rock with sulfuric acid.

synthetic fibers Textile fibers made by processing synthetic, plastic materials. Nylon was the original synthetic fiber.

Teflon The plastic polytetrafluoroethylene, known for its exceptional slipperiness.

thermoplastic A plastic that softens again when heated.

thermoset A thermosetting plastic; that is, a plastic which sets hard and rigid when molded and which does not soften again when heated.

turning A method of machining, carried out on a lathe.

TVP Short for textured vegetable protein, most familiar as a meat substitute made from soybeans.

unit operations Standard methods used to physically process chemical materials during manufacture. They include distillation, mixing, and filtering.

unit processes Standard chemical reactions carried out during chemical manufacture. They include oxidation, cracking, and polymerization.

vein A gap between rock layers that has become filled with minerals.

viscose The common form of rayon, consisting of pure cellulose fibers, which are regenerated from solution.

weaving Interlacing lengthwise (warp) and crosswise (filling, or weft) threads to make cloth. It takes place on a machine called a loom.

welding Joining together pieces of metal by means of fusion, or melting touching parts.

wood pulp The raw material for making paper, obtained by breaking down wood into fibers by means of grinding or chemicals.

Index

oxygen 17, 29

P

Pakistan 21, 25
palladium 10
panning 21, *21*
paper 8, 48, 78, 79
paperboard *19*
pasteurization 72
pencillin 76
Perkin W. H. 78, 80
permanent-mold casting 55
pesticides 70
petrochemicals 38, 40-43
petroleum 26, 38, 40, *43*
    refining of 42
pharmaceuticals 74, 77
phenol 40
pig iron 28, 30
placer mining 21
plastics 38, 39, 62, 66-68, *66, 67*
platinum 10
polyethylene 62, 66
polymerization 42, 63, 66, 68
polystyrene 66
polyvinyl chloride 38, 43, 66, *67*, 68
porcelain 36
potassium *16*
pottery 36
propellants 17
prospecting 14-15
pyrites 12

Q

quarrying 22
quartz 12
Queen Mary 54, *59*
quinine 77

R

railroads 82
ram 57
    hydraulic *57*
rayon 18
reforming 42-43
refractories 36, 37
resin 18
resistance welding 59
riffles 21
riveting 58, *58*
robots 51, 83
Rocket locomotive *49*
roller-spinning maching *50*
rolling 56

rolling mill *31*
room-and-pillar method 25
roundwood 19, *19*
rubber 18
rubber, synthetic 66
rust 10, 34, 35

S

saccharin 70
salt 25, 26, 27
sand 12, 28, 32
sand casting 55, *55*
satellites 14
Saudi Arabia 16
Savery, Thomas 49
screw-cutting lathe *49*
seawater 16, 20
seismic survey 14, *15*
shipbuilding 58, *83*
silica 12, 32, 37
silicon 83
silicon chips 51, 78, 83, 85, *85*
silk 69, 80
silk, artificial 65, 69
silver 10
slag 29, 31
smelting 29
sodium *16*, 34
sodium carbonate 64
sodium hydroxide 64, 65
softwoods 19
soldering 59
South Africa 8, 13, 20, 21
soybeans 74
space shuttle *17*
Spain 82
sphalerite 11
spinning 80
spinning jenny 49, *49*
spinning mule 49
stained glass *37*
stainless steel 35
stamping 57
steam cracking 43
steam engine *49*, 82
steel 28, 30, 35
steel casting *55*
steel plates 58, 59, *83*
steel rolling *48*
steelmaking 28, *54*
sulfur 26, 27
sulfuric acid 62, 64, 65
Sweden 11
synthetic drugs 77
synthetic fibers 69
synthetic food 74-75
synthetics 38-45

T

Teflon 38
textiles 49, 80-81
textured vegetable protein 74
Thailand 76
thermoplastics 66, 68
thermosets 66, 68
tin alloy 55
tin, smelting of 32
tools 7, 20
Trans-Alaska pipeline 26
triacetate 69
tungsten 60
turning 60

U

underground mining 24-25
unit operations 63
unit processes 63
United States 10, 17, 20, 22, 25, 38,
    49, 51, 59, 70
uranium 14, 28, 33

V

vacuum forming *68*
viscose 69
vitamins 74
volcanoes 12

W

water frame 49, *50*
Watt, James 49
weaving 80
weld, types of 58, *58*
welding 58, *58*
whisky 73, *73*
Whitney, Eli 49, 50
Wilkinson, John 49
wine production *52*
wood 7, 8, 18
wood pulp 8, 18, 19, 78, 79, *79*
wool 80

Z

Zambia 11
Zimbabwe 14
zinc 11
    smelting of 32, *33*
zinc alloy 55

Further reading

Aaseng, Nathan. *Better Mousetraps: Product Improvements That Led to Success.* Minneapolis: Lerner, 1989.

Bates, Robert L. *Industrial Minerals: How They Are Found and Used.* Hillside, N.J.:Enslow Publishers,1988.

Caney, Steven. *Steven Caney's Invention Book.* New York: Workman Publishing, 1985.

Dineen, Jacqueline. *Metals and Minerals.* Hillside, N.J.: Enslow Publishers, 1988.

Dineen, Jacqueline. *Plastics.* Hillside, N.J.: Enslow Publishers, 1988.

Fodor, R.V. *Gold, Copper, Iron: How Metals Are Formed, Found and Used.* Hillside, N.J.: Enslow Publishers, 1989.

Franck, Irene M., and David M. Brownstone. *Manufacturers and Miners.* New York: Facts on File, 1989.

Kolb, Kenneth E., and Doris K. Kolb. *Glass: Its Many Facets.* Hillside, N.J.: Enslow Publishers, 1988.

Macaulay, David. *The Way Things Work.* Boston: Houghton Mifflin Company, 1988.

Mercer, Ian. *Oils.* New York: Gloucester Press/Watts, 1989.

National Geographic Society. *Inventors and Discoverers: Changing Our World.* Washington, D.C.: National Geographic Society, 1988.

Natural History Museum Staff. *Rocks and Minerals.* New York: Alfred A. Knopf, 1988.

Pampe, William R. *Petroleum: How It Is Found and Used.* Hillside, N.J.: Enslow Publishers, 1984.

Parker, Steve. *The Marshall Cavendish Science Project Book of Mechanics.* London: Marshall Cavendish, 1988.

Smith, Elizabeth S. *Paper.* New York: Walker & Company, 1984.

Symes, R.F. *Rocks & Minerals.* New York: Alfred A. Knopf, 1988.

Whyman, Kathryn. *Metals and Alloys.* New York: Gloucester Press/Watts, 1988.

Whyman, Kathryn. *Plastics.* New York: Gloucester Press/Watts, 1988.

Whyman, Kathryn. *Rocks and Minerals.* New York: Gloucester Press/Watts, 1989.

Whyman Kathryn. *Textiles.* New York: Gloucester Press/Watts, 1988.

Picture Credits

	DATE DUE		